Not Born Here

Stories from Marsden, N.C.

Dennis Sinar

Not Born Here
Stories from Marsden, N.C.

by Dennis Sinar

Print Edition

Editions ISBN
Soft cover 9780991006816
PDF 9780991006823

LCCN 2014906734

This is a work of fiction, not intended to portray any individual,
living or dead. Names, characters, places, and incidents either are
products of the author's imagination or are used fictitiously.
Characters are a composite of personalities, expanded and molded
as needed.

Cover design by Dennis Sinar. Image of "Morning Memories"
used with permission of the artist, Doris Schneider.
Proofread by Tia Silverthorne Bach of INDIE Books Gone Wild
Published by Knowledgeworks123, Southport, N.C. 28461

Dedication:

To Kathryn, Evan, Emily, Avery and Hayden

The past, the present, and the future

Reviewer praise for Not Born Here

"Written by a Yankee but filled with southern charm, *Not Born Here* embraces the heart of southern culture and tradition with humorous and heart-warming stories. Sinar's characters jump off the page with telling details and the cadence of the south in an affectionate nod to his adopted home." Marni Graff, award-winning author of *The Nora Tierney Mysteries.*

"Excellent use of dialogue! When I read these stories I feel like I am sitting at Bojangles eating a cheese biscuit and listening to the locals talk over their morning cup of coffee. Sinar provides us with humorous, yet uncannily accurate narratives of life in a small Southern river town. I highly recommend this work to those who are considering retiring in the South or who just want an enjoyable read." Ross Hamory, former Marsden resident.

"Sinar captures the unique voice and rich color of yesterday's Coastal Carolina people, rivaling Patsy Moore Ginns's recounts of Carolina life in her book *Rough Weather Makes Good Timber*. Each unique story features characters from the fictitious town of Marsden who offer the reader a glimpse into their own unique life experiences. This is a witty, colorful preservation of local flavor, uniqueness and language spun by an accomplished storyteller." Angela Beach Silverthorne, award-winning coauthor of *Depression Cookies*

Dennis Sinar's *Not Born Here Stories from Marsden N.C.*, wraps one in the distinctive atmosphere of a leisurely Southern-style visit with the neighbors. The ambling pace of each unfolding biography offers the authenticity of oral history. The diversity of characters evokes both the simplicity and richness of human lives with their unexpected twists of fate and lessons learned. It is a pleasure to read. Holly Bull, President of the Center for Interim Programs.

"Dennis Sinar has written a charming book which, with its grace and tongue-in-cheek humor, does honor both to his studied Southern characters and to observers from north of the Mason-Dixon Line. You are sure to enjoy this romp through both cultures."
Jayne Davis Wall author of *Winter Goldfinch.*

"Dennis Sinar is a transplanted Yankee whose book, *Not Born Here*, captures the experience of a culture foreign to his own. He treats his characters and their stories with a relish and kindness, retelling them so that we can share the sounds, tastes, textures, and visuals that enrich the heritage we Southerners take for granted. You will smile, laugh aloud, and maybe find yourself in his characters and their attitudes toward life and home." Doris Schneider, author of *Borrowed Things.*

"A story is a way of preserving not only an incident in a life, but a manner of speaking and living. Dennis Sinar's stories, culled from Eastern North Carolina characters, are valuable because they ring true in their detail. Though their voices are fictionalized, we'd recognize any one of them from the patter hereabouts of overheard conversations and spontaneous confidences." Rachel Victoria Mills, teacher and artist.

Not Born Here, Stories from Marsden, N.C. by Dennis Sinar, is delightful. I enjoyed getting to know an eclectic mix of residents in this fictional Southern town. Their stories, both past and present, captured my imagination." Kay Wilson.

"North and South, the greater our differences, the more we are the same. Different accents, family backgrounds, and geographic locations - we are all searching for the same things - love, compassion, understanding, and sometimes relief from what ails us - the differences that make us the same. In *Not Born Here*, Sinar captures the similarities and differences in a style that makes us appreciate our neighbors."
Diane Bowen.

Acknowledgements

The people of Marsden are the inspiration for these
stories, and I hope I've captured their personalities and
love of life. Sincere thanks to members of the Pamlico
Writer's group and the River Walk Writers Group for
their encouragement and critique. It was gratifying to
know that one or another story rang true to their
experience. Special thanks to Barbara Rouse for her
encouragement and humor and for always being willing
to read another story. Thanks also to friends Doris
Schneider and Jayne Wall for their ideas, inspiration,
and encouragement and for their insightful critiques.

Contents

The People of Marsden

Stories from Marsden

Introduction

"I can tell a Yankee right off by whether he butters his bread after it's toasted or before."

I overheard this comment shortly after moving to Marsden. Such a simple difference in habits, but one that some claim divides half of the United States, separating North and South. Such a difference between Yankees and Southerners deserves looking into.

Being born in a place imparts a special allegiance. In contrast, moving to a place, especially later in life, lets you notice regional differences of the people and their customs. I was not born Southern, and have regretted that all my life. Living in the South later in life sharpens my images of southern people, specifically the people of coastal North Carolina, and more particularly, the people of Marsden.

This is a collection of stories about people in this part of the country, their views on life, on family, and on living in the South. The characters are a merging of many personalities; the people of Marsden and retirees transplanted to Marsden. These are stories from the people you'd meet on the street in any Southern town. Like many good stories, these start with a kernel of truth and expand a bit to fill in those details people might not share with an outsider. I welcome your comments on the format and the stories, and suggestions on additional stories that may need to be told.

Dennis Sinar

May 2014

Southport, North Carolina

The People of Marsden

Kate

I'm just a bit over eighty now and have lived in coastal North Carolina all my life. You asked for my story and I'm glad to tell it, but I want to warn you that I've lived inside a lot of stories and came through them to be the person I am today. Telling a story honestly when you've been inside it is colored by all of the person's past stories and by their remembrance of this story. Sometimes the story has some emotion with it that doesn't fade over time. My point is that for me, telling any story is complicated because I carry my emotions close to the surface. This story has a lot of personal emotion and I may tear up when I tell it, and you'll need to excuse any tears. The story I tell of the places and the times may not be entirely accurate as someone else might tell it, but it's how I remember it.

I grew up in Walstonburg on a small farm. Mom spent long days doing household chores because that's what was needed; dad was in the fields from dawn till late. When he came in, he picked right up doing things that needed to get done: chopping wood, repairing things, and tending to the sick animals. I was an only child and a girl, so dad had to do the extra work that a boy would do. I could help some, but my mom only let me do so many of the heavy chores.

We pumped water from the well for all our needs. It was good tasting water, nice and cool in the summer. I remember a long drink of well water as one of the best feelings for a thirsty kid on a hot summer day. When I was a small child, I don't recall having a refrigerator, but I recall the ice man coming every few days. About once a week we bought a big block of ice, and the ice man placed it in the shed because mom could not lift that much weight. The ice stayed covered in the shed with a burlap bag and I chipped off a chunk for whatever we needed. My momma used a washboard for the clothes and cooked all of our meals on a wood stove. We grew most of what we needed on our land and we canned the vegetables as they were harvested. As the old saying goes, if you can't grow it, you probably don't really need it. Meat came from our pigs, and we didn't eat much beef. Of course, we had chickens a plenty, and our eggs were what they now call 'free range' because those chickens were everywhere.

Pretty near every weekend in the fall there was hog killin. Families gathered with farm workers to prepare meat for the coming winter. The process involved four to five hogs, about all that the group could manage efficiently. There's a lot of meat on a hog and it needs to be handled correctly to avoid spoiling. After the hog was dispatched and carved up, the meat was smoked or salted to preserve it. I never saw the killin part since my dad kept me away from that. I sometimes had dreams about that hog running in the yard eating slop on one day and on the table in a week or so. I was assigned the girl's job of holding the chitterlings open so my momma could wash the excrement from the still-warm intestines. I don't think I'll ever forget the smell of fresh hog intestines, the steam rising from the endless pile on the table. Other people on our human assembly line took the cleaned chitterlings and held them open for stuffing as sausage casings. The sausage recipe was my dad's special one and he would not share it with anyone. Mom never wrote the recipe and I guess it's lost now.

What did we do for fun?

Other families visited in warm weather and the adults played cards, either Setback or Pitch. The adults would play for hours around the kitchen table laughing and talking about local farm news, crop prices, and small town gossip. Children played Old Maid, but we were expected to make it a quiet game. Children listened to the adults and laughed when they laughed, even though we may not have known what they were laughing about. There was no running around or shouting during adult card games or we'd get a swat after being pulled up short. Kids were expected to be quiet and respectful around adults, with *quiet* the most important word in that sentence.

As I got older, I worked in the fields looping tobacco. The men would walk along the row, pick the bottom leaves as they ripened and put them into sacks on their back. When the sacks filled up, they set them at the end of a row and picked up a new sack and someone came to take the full sacks back to the barn. That was a time for a short break when the sack was being changed, no more than five minutes. There were a lot of rows to harvest in a short time and the weather was always a worry. If it rained hard or hailed, the leaves might be ruined, especially the middle leaves that brought the highest prices.

Back then, doctors made house calls. My family was pretty healthy. It cost a lot of money to pay a doctor for his visit; but if you did not have money, he would take a trade of chickens and eggs and, occasionally, a ham or canned vegetables. It made me wonder how much food the doctor had around his house during a sickly season. Before she called the doctor, Mom tried her store of remedies. The things that worked for our ailments were mixtures she had either learned from her people or heard about from neighbors. Nearly every winter I'd get a dose of Vicks for a cold, smeared on my chest and neck and wrapped in a flannel rag to help magnify the effect. Somehow flannel had magical properties, because I was almost always better the next morning after a night of Vicks and flannel wrap. I never had my tonsils out, but one of my cousins did and had to go to Raleigh for the operation. Even though our doctors at the local hospital could take out tonsils, my cousin had a special case that needed an expert surgeon. We visited the big city to see him, and he acted proud and uppity to be there in a fancy bed with clean sheets.

My momma believed in the Watkins man. He came every month and delivered the things she'd ordered the previous month. In the 1940s, he came by railroad and walked to our house. Later he got an old Model A Ford with a horn that I loved because the "OOgha, OOgha" let us know he was coming. His visits were the high point of the day because Mom was excited about what he brought: his items and news of the outside world. He sold Pinee liquid and Cloverine salve for cuts and Mom bought a fresh supply about every year. If we got a cut, we smeared some salve on, wrapped the cut in a clean rag, and it never got infected. She also brought Grove's Chill Tonic occasionally. My mom felt she needed to keep that on hand in case I got really sick. I still recall the big aqua bottle in the cupboard with dust on it if everyone was healthy. My mom used a lot of castor oil, or at least I swallowed a lot of Castor oil. Neighbor kids told me it's not the taste that is so bad, but the smell. If you pinch your nose to block the smell, it has no taste. They emphasized that you washed your hands and lips so you don't get any smell sneaking in and making you feel queasy. Holding my nose always worked for me, so I never minded Castor oil. I hear that Walmart has a tasteless Castor oil for sale, but I've never tried it. I don't know how Mom handled the adults, but when I told her what was bothering me, she chose carefully between Pinee liquid, Cloverine salve, Vicks, or Chill

Tonic. Most often as the first line treatment she chose Castor oil.

We never had much cash around the house; we didn't need it because there was no-where to spend it. Mom kept what cash we had in small jars on the top shelf, some for the Watkins man, some for going to town, and some for emergencies. If dad went to town for supplies, she gave him the cash he'd need. Usually, he'd bring back a treat like a Mary Jane or Tootsie Roll. We never had the big bags of candy like we have now. Maybe those big bags are why everyone is so fat today. Most times the Watkins man would bring a sucker for me. Cherry was my favorite then and still is. Other people remember the Watkins man giving them a small color card with their purchase, but our Watkins man only had candy.

Back then, we did not have electricity in our house. It took some time for Walstonburg to get electric power. After we got electricity, we'd listen to the radio in the living room after the work had been done and before I had to go to bed. I fell asleep to the sound of the radio playing in the other room. Dad said that our house got electricity early because it was close to the road. It was expensive to pay to bring the line from the street to the house. For neighbors it took another year before they could afford the cost. It sounds corny now, but for years after we'd gotten electric lights, I studied by an oil lamp. It makes me think of the stories people tell about Abe Lincoln; but for me, the flickering light from an oil lamp was real, especially in the winter. The flickering lamp light never did seem to damage my eyesight. Even as old as I am, my eyesight has been sharp until recently when I got reading glasses.

Because I was an only child, I only saw other children at church or in school. In the summer when school was out, we hardly ever saw friends unless the child lived close enough to walk over to play. There was little enough time for idle play back then because most of the day was taken up with chores. Getting back and forth to another kid's house was a problem. Dad needed the truck for essential errands and kid visits were not essential. Girl sleep-overs were fun in the summer because of the novelty, but it was usually just one other girl. We were not allowed to sleep outside. Boys, usually cousins, played together a lot on Sundays around family dinner time. Adults expected quiet children. If we were fooling around outside, it had better be far away from the house.

Mom let me start dating in a group at sixteen and always at school functions. She would not let me go on a singles date with a boy. At about that age, I overheard Mom and another mother talking over cards one night. The other mom said something about avoiding trouble by girls being in a group, whatever they meant by trouble. I can't recall boys smoking or drinking beer on a date. We girls felt it was a sign of respect that our dates were courteous and well-behaved. We knew that the boys got together at their hangout after the date to drink and smoke, but I never saw any of that.

Of course, I got along well with my dad. He felt I was his special only child. Mom was more practical. As I got older, she was strict about what I wore in public. She didn't let me wear even a little makeup. Makeup was the fashion in the 1940s and it was not expensive, so she could afford a bit. Momma loved her makeup, putting it on carefully every morning with some foundation, Coty powder and finish, and some red lipstick. She did not have much free time during the day, so when she had a bit of leisure time, she used that extra time to put her makeup on slowly, experimenting with how it looked. She would put on a bit more Coty powder and a fresh coat of lipstick before Dad came in for dinner. She tried to look her best for him. As I got older, I preferred Avon makeup. The Avon lady had a bigger selection of colors, she came right to the door and let me try out the different colors. She was our source about how to look like the models we'd seen in the Sears catalog.

I met my husband when I was eighteen. He worked as a line construction man installing electric power to the farm houses in our area. He rented a room at my aunt's house down the road, and we met over dinner at her house one Sunday. I loved living at home; but when I got old enough and met my future husband, I knew it was time for me to be with him. After I got married, we visited home for Sunday dinner, but it was never the same. I started a new life and the old one was gone forever.

Bitsy

I grew up on the edge of town. It may sound strange in a place as small as Marsden, but my family's house was on the corner of the first unpaved road outside of town. The location was strategic for a kid growing up because everything was within walking distance. There was a big wrap-around porch on the front and sides where all the neighborhood kids gathered. It was a happy home, noisy with children's laughter. We were not poor, but not well off either. My dad's jobs changed every few years, and between jobs we might be a little more on the poor side. Somehow my mom managed our money so that we did not feel poor. She was a wonderful nurturing influence. Her simple philosophy: because we didn't have a lot, we had a responsibility to use our gifts as worthwhile people. In her mind, being worthwhile was better than having a lot of money.

Marsden was that idyllic small town where no one locked their doors and everyone knew each other. Neighbors watched out for children other than their own and told their parents if someone was doing something they should not be doing. The down side of that familiarity was that people knew too much about your business. I was an adventurous child with the run of the town, but I knew to tow a narrow line or someone might tell my parents. I never knew who might know my parents, so I tried to be courteous to all adults and behave like a worthwhile young lady. Some stranger on the street might see me spit on the sidewalk or cross the street without looking and I would only find out later at home under my mother's stare.

I went to school at St. Agnes, the Catholic school on Market Street. St. Agnes was a small school and close to home. All the neighborhood kids walked to school in a cluster. Your walking companions changed by age and current friendships. School was an easy walk from my house; of course, back then, walking at any time of day was expected. Classes were small and the school often split classes with two grades in the same room taught by one nun. That schedule offered a fair amount of independent work time while the other class had the teacher's attention. Strict silence was enforced to not disturb the other class. Anyone who's been taught by Catholic nuns knows there was not much tolerance for disruptive talking or other silliness. Parents were the enforcers, and the teacher was an extension of your parents, to be obeyed. A note sent home by the teacher meant trouble from my parents. When I grew up, the Catholic Church was about ritual and pageantry, a sense of order and punishment for variation. Those qualities seemed to be stabilizing influences on young children. There was a black Catholic Church and school across town, Mother of Mercy, but we hardly ever saw those children. It was just that way in Marsden.

Religion has always been important to my family, but our religion was based in the home, not the Catholic Church. We had a home church service every Sunday morning at my grandparent's house, and my grandfather led the informal service with readings and silent prayer. Family was expected to be on time, the children shiny clean and neatly dressed. My family were not singers; but my grandfather loved music, so he had my grandmother play church hymns on the record player for special occasions. My dad was not a church person, but he went for my mother. Mom worried a lot that my dad had never been baptized. One Sunday they went off for a walk after the service, and she had a talk with him about heaven and baptism. She told me the story with tears in her eyes. She told him that she loved him, and that when they died, she wanted to be with him forever in heaven. That could not happen if he wasn't baptized, because souls that were not baptized could not go to heaven. He was baptized the next Sunday, and she was proud that she had saved his soul. Mom told me that story the night before I got married. I guess it was her way of showing a personal example of marital love.

After the new public school was built I changed schools for the eight grade, and I had to adjust to new friends like everyone does. A typical small town discussion at the beginning of the school year started with; "What does your father do?" The answer to that question labeled your social class for the rest of your time in that school.

We had a maid, even though we were not well off. Maryella did not live with us, but came early each morning to help my mom and tend to the children. Most of the neighbor women had help around the house. Relationships between black people and white people back then were classic examples of Southern tradition. As an example, when our Maryella died, my mom took food to her family and gave them some money. She talked for days about how Maryella's house was so clean, cleaner than ours. I was surprised because, after all, she was our maid and kept our house clean. In one of his jobs, my dad supervised several black men at the garage. One year, dad got sick enough to be in the hospital. Several of his black employees came to visit him in the hospital to wish him well, and he was surprised that they would come all the way to the hospital to visit him. One morning, I found a black man in a military uniform asleep on our porch. Mom gently shook him awake and gave him a cup of coffee. He drank it sitting on the porch, thanked her, and went on his way on the road out of town. She told me he'd probably had a bit too much to drink and just needed a place to sleep. To her, our porch was as good a place as any. People had a different sense of trust in Marsden at that time.

Maryella was an excellent maid according to Momma and was authorized to give any of the children a good swat if they deserved it. Maryella had her beliefs in health and disease, and they seemed strange to me. She wore what she called a cunja bag around her neck day and night to ward off disease. It had a soft powder in it and smelled terrible. Maybe it worked because we never saw her sick. Like many people in that time, she smoked and rolled her own cigarettes because they were cheaper that way. I recall one spring I had an ear infection and she put me on my side and blew cigarette smoke into one ear and then the other. The pain in my ear was better by morning. I did not get sick much; but when I got a sore throat that went on for more than two days, my mom told me to walk over to the old Fowler Hospital, where the fire station is now, and tell the doctor it was okay for him to give me a shot of Penicillin. Penicillin shots always seemed to go deep enough to scrape the bone in my skinny arm. After the shot, my sore throat got better in a day or so. I occasionally got a painful reisen on my arm after a bug bite. Mom would rub some black smelly salve on it, and the infection was drawn out by morning. It never scarred.

Polio was a scare for all families of the time. Every fall, we listened to the town gossip about whether there was Polio in our part of North Carolina. When news came from the doctors that the disease was in town, the police closed the movies and the swimming pools. Meetings and church gatherings were canceled to stop people from spreading the disease. I don't recall being vaccinated, although I'm sure I was.

Mrs. Jolly's grocery store was close, just a block away towards town. I loved to stand in front of the big candy case and think long and hard about how to spend my nickel. It usually went for Mary Jane's, six of them for a nickel. I was disciplined enough to only eat two slowly when I got out of the store and saved the rest for later. At Jolly's, we had a credit account that mom paid every week after my dad gave her his pay. During hard times, Mrs. Jolly was kind enough to let our credit extend a bit until Dad found a new job. My mom used to call that being "financially embarrassed." She was a sound financial manager, even during tough times, I don't remember wanting for any necessities.

For weekend entertainment we went to the movies downtown. The Reita Theater ran Saturday morning movies for kids. Admission was twelve cents if you were less than twelve years old and jumped to a quarter if you were over twelve. The little gray-haired ticket lady had a magical gift for telling when a kid had passed the eleventh year. I can still see her staring down at me through her glasses, her gray hair curled tightly around her ears. The Reita ran cowboy serials because they drew a consistent crowd; but if you missed a week, you missed out on major parts of the story. Friends might give you a quick update, but it was not the same as watching in person. If you missed more than a week, it was not worth going again until they started a new serial. After the serial there were a few cartoons, and then a full-length cowboy feature starring Roy Rodgers or Gene Autry. The main theater was across the street from the Reita and mostly showed musicals and comedies for adults. On those few times we got to go to an adult movie, it was usually on a Sunday afternoon. Afterwards Mom and Dad liked to go to Adams Soda Shop right next to the theater for a milkshake.

The Bug House was gone by then and a brick Recreation Center replaced it. Any kids that came to the Center got free dance lessons in square dancing, slow dancing and most importantly be-bop. Today be-bop is known as the shag, but we never called it that. Rock and roll was just coming on the radio and fast dances were the most fun. Back then, boys were great dancers. I loved to dance and had more than my share of boys asking me. There was a great chili place on the edge of town with the best chili dogs. Plain and simple: a dog, a soft warm bun, some mustard, and the best chili ever. There were contests of who could eat the most dogs the fastest without spilling a drop of chili. As a teen, I got to the other entertainment places in town by piling into someone's car and headed down toward the river to the St Moritz, a teenage hang out for dancing and cheeseburgers. The big difference between the townies and the country kids was that country kids hung out further down the road at the little store at the "Y" for their cheeseburgers.

In high school, there was a big social difference between the townies and the country kids. The townies got all the attention, and were the class officers, cheerleaders, and band members. A few of the bigger country boys got onto the football or basketball teams in years when we needed muscle and speed. As I got older, girls had pajama parties and boys came to visit early, but left in plenty of time for us to enjoy girl talk about who we thought was cute or a good dancer. Boys were always courteous on dates and never drank or smoked.

Entertainment and food were popular themes in our church, and a cake walk was a favorite social event for women. A cake walk started with a large circle drawn on the floor with numbered squares inside the circle. When you bought a ticket, you got a paper with a number on it. Your number went into a container for the drawing. All the people who had a ticket walked around the circle as music plays. When the music stopped, a number was drawn. If it was the square you were standing on, you won the cake. Cake walks were usually fundraisers held before Thanksgiving so that your family could have a nice dessert for a special Thanksgiving dinner. The tradition in Marsden was to put your recipe below the cake. Everyone knew who made the best cakes, but those women would not give out their recipes. If you bought a cake that did not have a recipe, you knew it was going to be good. Bake sales showcased a woman's talent in an era when homemaking skills were valued. It was an embarrassment if you made a cake and did not see it out on display for sale. I went to a bridge lunch one Wednesday and overheard someone at an adjacent table talking about the poor quality of a coconut cake they bought at a cake walk. It was my mom's cake, I was sure of it. She never baked that cake again.

I've lived in many parts of the country with my family, but always felt my home was Marsden. The place has changed. Then again, it hasn't. The spirit of the Southern people seems the same, or maybe I'm just used to it. There seem to be a lot more retirees who have settled here, and most of them seem to be from the north. Their style is different, more abrupt and less gentle. They always seem to be in a hurry.

TOB

You asked me to tell you about living at the river. Well, you've lived here for some time, so you know a little bit of what it's like. But maybe you're more interested in how it used to be, kind of the good 'ole days.

When I came to the river, it was a pretty isolated place, and everybody liked that isolation. I moved to Marsden with my family as a child of fourteen. One cold February night our house burned to the ground when a stray ash from the fireplace caught the rug on fire. We could not save much. We moved from the country to the outskirts of Marsden. Land was cheap and we had nothing after the fire. In the beginning, the best my daddy could afford was an old trailer, but it was ours. Most of the places around were fishing cottages for well-to-do people from the city, doctors and such. Simple places really, high on stilts because of flooding. The fancy ones had indoor toilets and county water. Back then, women and children came to stay for the summer, and the men worked in the city and came down for the weekend. In the other seasons the men would use the places for fishing or duck hunting. You didn't see folks much except in the summer, or on weekends and holidays. They were city folks, and although we liked for them to come, we liked it better when Monday came and they all went back to their real homes and left things quiet again.

But I expect you want me to get back to my story. Potatoes were a good crop for the farmers, and there was steady work for anyone who wanted it. I worked the potato harvest in Aurora for two seasons. In the middle 1940s from June to August, 120 railroad cars a day of potatoes moved out of here and across the country. The railroad went down to the waterfront in downtown Marsden, about where the present dock master's office sits. There was a wide wooden wharf along the water for loading goods going in and out by ship. At that time there was a popular oyster house across the water. I don't recall the name, but it was close enough to the bridge to walk to it from there. Good oysters, salty, and so big you had to chew to get one down.

After I came back from the war, I worked as a station agent and telegraph operator for the railroad because I'd learned the telegraph in the navy. Lucky for me there was a close similarity between navy signaling and railroad signaling, so it was easy to learn the railroad way. It was a good job when jobs were hard to come by. I worked that job for thirty-seven years in Marsden and retired when they closed Belhaven as a station. They offered me a job in Illinois, but I decided not to move cross country. I found work in town, another steady job with enough money to raise my family. I moved from downtown back out here to the river because land was still cheap, and it was a good place to raise my family of boys. Lots of space to explore and learn about the water. I built my place by hand in three months with the help of some friends. Lots back then were usually seventy-five feet of waterfront and extended back to the street. Nearly every lot had old pilings from piers that had washed away in storms, and it was cheap to just rebuild the pier if the pilings were good. Floods have always been a problem and maybe that's why the lots were so cheap. Fishing cottages on stilts are one thing in a flood, but a house built on the ground is another. My house has been flooded seven times, sometimes with two or three feet of water in the living room. At first we stayed during the storm, watched the water rise gradually over the road, then watched the power go out. The darkness and the helplessness are the worst. My boys were young during the first storm. At first they thought it was fun, using candles and watching the water get higher. Then the oldest got nervous and asked how we would get to safety and the rest started to panic. I sent my wife and the boys to the top floor and told them to pray. The water kept rising and it was dark everywhere and what candles we had kept going out. The railroad kerosene lamp was the only light we had. I worked with my brother to lift furniture up as high as I could, but the water kept coming, eventually soaking all the furniture. Finally, we just gave up, let the water come, and went upstairs with the family to wait it out. My wife said we would never stay again. In storms now, we leave before the water gets over the road.

I've raised the house above the flooding level after each storm and guess that's enough, but Mother Nature always seems to prove me wrong. Hopefully I'll not see it flooded again in my lifetime, but none of that is my decision. After a big storm, people slowly come back to see the damage, the high water, the destroyed pier, the floating debris. One old timer told me he worried most about snakes, the poisonous kind. He claimed snakes were displaced from their homes just like people, and they swam in the water in none-too-good a mood. He said that an angry copperhead or water moccasin can cause serious damage to someone walking in the water after the storm. Rubber boots are no real protection against that kind of snake bite. All that sounds pretty grim doesn't it? A storm is a nasty event for sure and luckily we only have them once a year or less, but they disrupt things. The same old timer that told me about the snakes, said storms were our payment for living in such a beautiful place. The flooding after a storm is not only a mess to clean up, it's smelly. River water soaking your stuff makes a smelly, dirty mess and so it's best to get things up and out of the water or throw it out. Flood insurance is expensive, so I never believed in it for my house here. Maybe that's a mistake, but I can't afford to pay that insurance bill when it will only get bad every so often. Overall, though, it seems to me like this spot on the creek has been lucky in most storms.

The worst hurricane for us was Hazel in 1954, the highest water and the most damage to the houses, at least in my area of the river. The way things are going, I'm not sure I'll see a last time for flooding. The weather people tell us their guesses of when floods will happen, but I think it's a magical combination of wind, wet ground from hard rain, and the time of a tide. It's hard to predict when a storm will cause flooding, because the storm changes speed and direction so quickly. If you've got your stuff on the ground, you have to move it to higher ground. Lately, weekend people have been pulling their boats and jet skis up along the road above the last water line. If you live at the river for any length of time, you learn to keep things up during hurricane season.

Out here, about 1949, the paved road ended at the Y. There was a hot dog stand and a small store for local people that sold a few basic items. On many a steamy summer day, I remember dipping some tongs in jar on the counter to find the pickle or egg I wanted to go with a hot dog and a cold drink. There was considerable change left from a dollar even after paying for all that food. After the store, this road was a dirt track. The marina was built about 1950 or so and the country club followed after that.

There was another hot dog stand closer to downtown that was flooded again and again and changed owners at least three times. They rent bikes and kayaks now. The family that owned the hot dog stand lived in the house and walked to work. The whole family worked the hot dog stand. Their specialty was chili dogs with a special chili recipe that made you want to eat more than one and wash it down with a cold drink.

The water in front of my house used to be crystal clear, maybe murky after a storm. After flooding from one or another hurricane, the government dug a canal somewhere downstream to help drain the tobacco fields. The fields had flooded especially bad that year and had ruined the crop. Tobacco was king then. I believe that since those drainage canals were dug, the dirt and muck and fertilizers and hog waste and who knows what else washed down into the creek when it rained to make it muddy and dirty all the time. The rains and storms continued, and with all that runoff of mud and sand from the canal, the creek was getting too shallow to get a boat up the creek from the mouth of the point. The government came back to dig a channel down the middle of the creek to allow small boats to come in without draggin bottom, and that's the channel we have today. Some of the best farmland soil in the county is at the bottom of the creek, washed down from floods and heavy rains.

I started fishing part time when I was on the railroad. The fish were plentiful in the creek and river, but there were no oysters, fished out years before. The inside breakwater at Belhaven was said to be full of big salty oysters for the taking around the 1950s. When I started fishing you could string your nets across the creek each night for two to three weeks at a time and the nets would hardly get dirty. Now, with all the mud in the river, they get so dirty after a day you have to spend more time cleaning them than you do processing any fish you catch. Clean nets are important to a fisherman; it's a sign of quality work.

Fishing is hard work. A typical day for a fisherman starts at daylight by placing nets. Back then nets were twenty-five yards long and legally could be staked across the broad part of the creek during nighttime, but were not allowed in the channel during daylight hours. The nets were staked in place on either end. A good net stake should be about the diameter of your arm from a straight sixteen foot tree. Where I worked, the river is not deep. Good stakes last a long time and are hard to come by; wood strong enough and thick enough to set well into the bottom and hold the net when it's full of fish. Cleaning and repairing nets took a lot of time then, but now nets are so cheap you don't clean them, you just buy a new one.

Everyone says it, so I'll just repeat it here: fishing and crabbing are off because of too many people taking too many fish and crabs. That over-fishing and changes in the river water quality don't let the crabs grow as well. My son, who works the river and is as good at fishing as most people, has more time off during the year for the last ten years when fishing is not making money. He's been able to find work sorting crabs at the seafood stores. He got frustrated a few years and gave up net fishing and now just does crabbing, but works harder because he as to spend extra time power washing his crab pots. I'm telling you there is a lot of maintenance in the business and time is money; so, if you spend more time maintaining your tools than catching fish or crabs, you lose money.

Making a living for my family as a fisherman was comfortable because I had several strapping boys to help me. People ask what's it like to fish for a living? My answer is a simple one. If you're finishing for fun, it's just that—fun. You can quit when you get tired. If you fish for a living, it's hard physical work and you have to push on even if you're tired, the weather's bad, or your nets are torn by careless boaters, not to mention when the fish aren't running, or when your boat is acting up. If the fish are running, and you have a cold, you better be out there in whatever weather, hoping you don't get too sick.

What tips do I have for fishing in the river? That's simple. Go to the local tackle shop and hang out. Listen to the people talk about what is running and what bait they use to catch fish. Those people are in the business of knowing and they will share their knowledge if you're patient. Some of the time they will even be right. When you first come in the store, they know you're a stranger, and conversation may stop. Don't take that personally, it's just their way. Best to listen to the chatter a bit and then politely ask your question. Most times the person who speaks up first is not necessarily the brightest one, so get plenty of opinions and decide for yourself before you buy anything.

What social life there was at the river was family oriented. When TV came, we would all go down to the house of someone who had a TV and watch the programs. The shows mostly were on weekend nights. On a good night, you could pick up Norfolk and the Red Skelton hour. That was a funny show with none of those dirty jokes that are so common on TV now. On most nights the reception was terrible; there was no picture but you could hear the program just fine. It was like radio with fuzz on the screen. TV reception at the river has always been lousy, for so long until we got cable. With cable the reception is better, but the programs are terrible.

You asked me for my favorite fish stew recipe. Honestly, I don't eat fish stew, never cared for it. I like a fish baked, or occasionally fried, but not in a stew. There are plenty of good rock stew recipes and maybe you can find one that someone will share. Rockfish is the best fish for stew.

He sat back in his chair and looked out over the water as our talk was coming to an end. I asked for his thoughts on the best and worst times at the river. He thought a bit and spoke as he ended a rock cycle. The worst time is during a storm. The water is rising, the power is out, it's dark and windy, and you don't know how long it's going to last. It's scary to be alone with your family way out here.

And the best time? All the rest of the time.

Roger

Patrice and I moved to Marsden to retire from South
Boston almost twenty years ago. Although we've been
here for years, we are still outsiders.

I grew up in a stable Christian home in a small Boston
suburb. Christianity and moral values were important to
my parents, and so we attended church every Sunday
and participated in church social activities. My father
was a factory worker while my mother was an efficient
manager of our home. Her envelopes for each budget
category were filled and emptied as payday and bills
came. This was before the credit card era, and Mom
preferred the certainty of cold cash. She mailed the
occasional check to a catalog supply house, but our town
was small enough that she could pay monthly bills in
cash and in person.

We were not rich; lower middle class would be our
demographic today. We knew of rich families in our
small town, but they were a class apart. The prominent
families in our town were sensible old rich; they were
the town leaders, used to having money, holding money,
spending money, and most importantly, growing money.
We lived in a world apart from those people, but mom

worked to model their lives in our frugal, yet comfortable, lifestyle. She'd send me on my bike to the local grocer to get a pound of ground beef and wanted me to pay him precisely the amount she gave me, not a penny more or less. That required the butcher to adjust his patty several times to the money I had been given.

During most summers, my parents passed me to a childless aunt and uncle for long visits. Both were doting and nurturing because I was not there long enough to much disrupt their quiet country life. My Aunt Ellen was quiet and supportive, but had an inner toughness from growing up as an only girl among seven brothers, and I admired that quality. Those grand childhood summers passed lazily with light chores around the house, a small allowance, and plenty of lakes and woods to explore. It's easy to enjoy life if you're the center of attention.

I am a maker of lists, because organization and completeness are easier with a list. Long ago when my mom was sending me off to college, I found my lists from childhood carefully hidden in my secret place in the basement. I reread them carefully, reviewing what had been on my mind then. Surprisingly, the same thoughts are still on my mind today: why we are here and how to make a mark in the world. The lists summarized my childhood beliefs that people made their own way in the world, earned a salary by a fair day's work, saved what they earned, spent wisely, and gave a small amount to those less fortunate than themselves.

My only sister was getting to an age to want to wear makeup. I overheard when she shyly asked Mom if she was pretty. Mom's reply was pragmatic: that beauty takes work and to be beautiful, women have to suffer to carry it off. She continued that men didn't need to work to be beautiful, because they had power.

Mom had a stock of old flannel shirts cut into long strips for use during cold season. Her stockpiling cotton for our sore throat therapy started with diapers. As we got to teens, she exhausted diapers and turned to dad's old shirts. To her, flannel had magical properties, magnified when applied to a sick person's neck or chest with a good swab of Vicks. She was practical, especially when it came to illness and medicine. When word got around the neighborhood that a kid had any childhood illness, she'd send us down the street to play with them for the day. Sure enough, about a week later we had it. She believed in natural immunity. At school time, she sent me on my bike to the doctor's office to tell them I needed my immunizations updated.

Mom thought she needed to do everything to maximize our immune defenses, so she regularly fed each of us (unknown to us) a tablespoon of dirt every month. She confessed this practice when I was home from college and complaining of a runny nose. Her technique was to gather scoops of dirt from clean open fields around the city and store it in a quart jar. And some time during the month, she pulled out a hefty spoonful and mixed it in our food so that we hardly noticed the grit. Truth was that if we noticed, we knew better than to complain about it. She admitted it was a practice her grandmother had brought over from the old country. It had worked for several generations and she was not going to break the string of good medical practice. My grandmother constantly wore a bag of herbs around her neck as a preventative. She called it a cunja bag and it smelled so badly that all of the children avoided hugging her. My Internet search suggests that wearing a cunja bag was a common practice to prevent illness in Eastern Europe. Bags of herbs worn around the neck were used as a preventative in the worldwide Spanish flu epidemic of 1918. There must have been a lot of home remedies in that year of the deadliest epidemic of all time with over 600,000 killed in America and over 50 million people killed worldwide. The herb combination in the bag varied by country, but the most common herb was the foul-smelling asafetida. Today the herb is commonly used in Middle Eastern cooking and is sold to promote digestive health.

My father was a quiet, supportive man who loved the mechanical order of household appliances and tools. When any appliance stopped working, he'd take it apart and study the wires and gears that functioned together to make the machine work. Usually, he could repair it. I watched him after he disassembled the appliance, staring at the pieces on the table, integrating the scattered parts into the whole, assessing functions and deducing the malfunctions. He worked this magic without the machine running, and I found that even more miraculous. Replacement parts were less common then, so he often had to find a discarded model at the dump, remove the good part, and replace it in our appliance. Mom was always frustrated by the collection of cannibalized appliances on his workbench. His smile when the appliance ran again was his reward.

We had a dog named Pete, named after the Our Gang comedy dog. Ours was a hyperactive dachshund. Pete played well with children and was smart enough to get out of the way when play got too rough. Pete started to get sick when I was eleven and gradually lost his energy, bladder and bowel control, and stopped eating. My mom debated long and hard before finally taking him to the vet. The vet diagnosed "cancer" and Pete came home to die. Mercifully one morning, Pete was dead, and I suspect Mom was sad that none of her remedies would help. We buried him in the backyard, even though it was winter and the ground was frozen. Dad lit a fire and thawed the ground enough so that we could dig a shallow grave. Pete was entombed in the cold ground. Pete dying was my first exposure to death. The memory that sticks even today is the coldness of the ground as we shoveled the frozen earth over him. I tear up a bit telling this story, and hope that he is reincarnated in a better place than Boston in the winter.

When college time came, my parents waved me off on the morning train into the city and on to Milwaukee. I was left to my own devices to get settled on the other end. I had two large suitcases that contained all that I owned: books, clothing and awards. My mom and dad did not plan on my coming back except to visit, so they packed everything and sold the rest. I was the first person in the family to go to college, and neither of them understood the procedure for sending a child to college. I had long been considered responsible. Settling in at college and doing well was my expected responsibility. Before I left, my mom gave me basic housekeeping training, such as sewing buttons, laundry, and ironing. She was training me for my future wife, she explained, so that I could help around the house. She leaned hard on the lesson that I must not look like a typical single man, disheveled and unbuttoned.

My early work history consisted of swinging between office jobs that were either tedious or promised profit from an untapped market. Dutifully performing repetitive tasks in the same cubicle always sapped my energy. For most of my career I have been selling products on the road, exploring new markets and the thrill of the new deal. Road sales are all about the thrill of looking into someone's eyes and judging their negotiating savvy in that initial split second. I miss that most of all. Over the ten years or so that I did road sales I got to know my regular customers as well as characters in a serialized novel, as keenly as needed to make the sale. Later I started comparing customers to the caricatures in a Jackie Gleason sketch, some bunglers, some ripe for an easy profit, and some with a harder edge, but each one a tough business character in their own mind.

I learned most from my first boss, who was an aficionado. Business was his life, and he was good because he worked at learning and advancing his business, and his moral mandate was to right the wrongs of society through his contact with customers. Every day, every encounter was a skirmish against unseen forces that prevented customers from buying his product to increase their well-being and happiness. I learned some of his cleverness by watching his eyes—burning, observant eyes, always gathering information about how his customers processed information. In a crowd of sales people, his quiet intensity at the edge of the crowd would be overshadowed by the bravado of others, but he was always gathering useful information. He was a man of efficiency, and did not like even a second of his time wasted by petty requests, or meaningless chatter. He sold whatever stuff there was to sell. We got on well because I respected his time. I'd come to his desk, make my report of sales progress, and he would smile knowingly and nod once only, ever efficiently using his energy. As I turned to leave, his eyes followed me to the door: whether out of distrust or admiration, I never could tell. As I closed the door, I once glanced back and saw his eyes were closed, but the same knowing smile remained on his face. In those days I had a plain honest face, simple even, and that was an advantage in the sales business. People often made the mistake of judging me as simple. I called on customers with a nondescript, vague smile, dressed in nondescript clothes that were neither stylish nor fancy. It helped my image if my coat and pants were a size too large and somewhat worn, giving the hint I might have gotten them from some discount store.

In my second job, I was more than a beginner with some experience in sales and the products our company sold, but not yet an expert with an established territory or sales persona. I played the part and passed among friends and colleagues as a successful salesman. From discussions, colleagues knew I had experience, and came to me for suggestions on their problems. Work days blended together in a pleasant mix. I had no need to look beyond a few days in the future to know my schedule, and never found myself looking back more than a few hours. I was so in love with work that I had trouble remembering what I'd eaten for breakfast or lunch. My mantra in sales: the soul of good business is to convince people to buy neither what they need nor what they can afford, but what's on special.

My career in sales was humming along when I started to look for companionship. I met Patrice at a church function, a singles dance I think. I was going to church regularly at that time. She was the prettiest girl there, and when I'd seen her in church, she always seemed at ease talking with men or women. I knew from the first time I saw her that I wanted to marry her. She had on a comfortable loose-fitting summer dress and open-toed red sandals. It was a casual dance, and her sandals made it hard for her to fast dance, but she managed. The music was provided by a church member who had a tape recorder with popular songs of the 60's. That era had songs you could dance to or just enjoy standing around and listening. I met her at the punch table. She had come off the dance floor to get punch, and smiled at me. I introduced myself and we shook hands. Her handshake was firm and she looked directly at me with shining eyes, a sign of confidence that I admired. We started small talk, and I found out this was her first church dance. Her broad smile highlighted her straight white teeth. She wore her soft blond hair long at her shoulders with a bright red ribbon. After these many years, I can still call up the way she looked, so at ease and comfortable, and so approachable.

Patrice had an air that night, not exactly an air of beauty, but an air of uniqueness. She impressed me as a treasure of a woman from her smiling face to her casual clothes, a woman in charge of herself and comfortable with her future. I asked her out to dinner and as our relationship progressed. We reveled in the happy times of new lovers; bliss in doing nothing but sitting together holding hands, walking in silence, feeling the other next to you, and wishing it not to end.

She gave up something intangible when she married me. I've never been able to define it. To her credit, she does not show any sign of having stepped down a notch to be with me. Inside, she is a better person than I; outside she acts to compliment me in any way she can. As I grew to know her more deeply, she impressed me as pragmatic and expressive. She has encouraged me to tell these stories- because she knows it is important to me, and I thank her for that gift.

Living in Marsden we discovered local characters, and even though we're Yankees, they treat us graciously. Emet Kelly is a neighbor and my source for local gossip about Marsden. He knows interesting people and tells a good yarn. Emet, or as he prefers, Met, makes it his business to watch over the comings and goings in Marsden. When he stopped over the day we moved in, he started the conversation with the typical Marsden expression, "You're not from around here are ya?" That opening line is almost universal in the South when meeting someone new, but I'd never heard it in Boston. It opens the conversation to explore any areas of your previous life, employment and heritage that may come up. It is not meant as a prying question, but rather an open-ended introduction. Met is tall and lanky and favors a cross between a bent straw and the scarecrow in the Wizard of Oz. He prefers a one-piece coverall outfit. The color of the coveralls change between blue and beige, but the style is the same. He wears a white shirt beneath the coveralls, long sleeve in winter and short sleeve in summer. He has a resonant tenor voice punctuated by a strong Carolina accent, interrupted by frequent throat clearing sounds, as if talking stretches his vocal cords. During conversations, I notice a dry cough

from his years of smoking Camels. There is usually a
stump of an unfiltered cigarette stuck to his bottom lip.
It does not come loose as he tells his stories. Recently
he's tried to stop smoking, so the Camel is unlit. To add
to his distinctiveness, he has projectile ears—ears
created by God for supporting a hat. He wears a baseball
cap, indoors or out, and his choice of hats extends from
a well-worn red cap from the NC Tobacco Growers to a
faded blue denim one from the Durham Bulls. The brim
is worn and stained from hard use. I never saw him
without a cap. Of course on that first meeting, Met
explained his name, because people always asked. His
given name is Emet. His mother had been to a circus
around the time of his conception, and after the circus
performance one thing led to another. She felt it would
be a good omen to name him after the great circus
clown, Emmett Kelly.

"Well, I ain't no clown," he says in no uncertain terms.
"And I've been trying to live that name down all my
life. I made up the Met part when I was a kid as a way
for other kids to leave the clown thing alone. Met's
stuck for these sixty or so years. People get it wrong all
the time, either thinking I can't spell or that they
misheard me. But by the time I correct them a few times,
I expect they remember the name."

Met prides himself on being on the sunny side of the IQ
curve. He considers himself intelligent and clever and
feels that's a practical combination. The clever part is
different than big-city clever, but effective in the small

town of Marsden. It's hard to get something over on him. He has a firm handshake from a lifetime of hard labor, and bright eyes from a lifetime of curiosity. His eyes see much more than they let on, as is often the case with clever people. He smiles easily and often, mostly at his own stories, congratulating himself on a particularly witty expression. He favors the Southern speech of a dropped g at the end of words such as livin', choppin', and eatin'. In Marsden, it's natural to adopt that shorthand speech. He is incapable of doing more than one thing at a time, and he finishes one thing before starting another; all in slow motion. He moves so slowly that it's tempting to help him along. His knowledge of local customs has been invaluable as we learn Southern customs. Before I start any new adventure in Marsden, I check with Met for the local protocol. He's not failed me, although he's had us do some pretty strange things. Like that time at our first pig pickin' when he told us we had to bring our best silver utensils. He cautioned us to be sure to keep the fork clean, so we brought a fresh towel and wiped the fork each time before we speared a new section of pig. Another of his tricks was to advise Patrice to stir a banana pudding three times in a clockwise direction before eating it for good luck. You get the picture of Met, a jokester in coveralls. Here is his story.

Met

I was born in coastal Carolina on a small farm, out close to where that fancy development is north of town. The tracks for the Norfolk and Southern ran right by the back of our house. Growing up, I could hear the train coming down the tracks, twenty or so cars filled with logs from up around Plymouth. The tracks were so close to our backyard, my daddy could come and go pretty much as he needed to. I had to laugh because someone downtown asked me what my daddy's job was on the railroad. He did not *work* on the railroad: he just rode the rails from one place to another looking for a handout. He'd come back every week or so to visit Momma and give her some of what he'd collected. Back then the railroads were an important way for poor folks to get around. One of my daddy's stories from when he was a child was about making a trip to Norfolk to visit family; the train to Jamesville, then a steamer upriver to Plymouth, another steamer over to Edenton, and finally catching the Norfolk and Southern to Norfolk.

As the smaller railroads merged around 1904, the steamer service from Jamesville to Plymouth was discontinued and the trip was a lot easier on one line. He smiled when he told the story because those were his well-off times. Now all he could afford was the freight lines in an unlocked boxcar. It was rare that a railroad cop would inspect his freight car, and even if they turned him out, he'd catch the next train that went by.

Our family had the farm for years, but sold it when developers offered a good price for the land. Most of the money went to pay off debts. I was raised on that farm and learned most of the important lessons of life from working the land. Anyone who's grown up on a farm knows what I mean: life and death, good luck and bad luck, cold winters and hot summers, always waiting for money from the crops.

My family never traveled when I was a child. The longest trip I can remember was a trip to Greenville in a neighbor's car. I don't know why we went, just that my parents spent some time at a bank while I wandered around the streets. When they came out, Momma was crying and Daddy had his arm on her shoulder, patting it. Maybe I was ripe to get in a bit of traveling as I got older. I felt things were starting to hum for me at about fifteen. I had girls looking at me and giggling when I walked by. They were local girls, plain and simple, but I loved the attention. There wasn't any money, and there was no place to spend it anyway. At the local store everyone knew everyone else; if I wandered into the store and talked to a girl, the story got back to my momma and she kidded me about it. I walked around with a cloud of embarrassment over my head most of the time, embarrassed about my height, my skinniness, and my clothes. The attention from those local girls told me they noticed me as different from the other boys my age and they thought there might be something special there. Of course those thoughts were too deep for me at that age, but I liked the feeling of them giggling as I walked past. I slumped down and scuffed the ground as I passed to show them I was aware of them, and I occasionally smirked in their direction.

I left Marsden at sixteen and found a job with a carnival. Farm work was boring and I was looking for adventure. The traveling carney came to town at country fair time. I got friendly with one of the guys running the wheel and asked him about the carney life and the pay. He said they were both as good as you made them. He introduced me to the manager, and I left town with them. I liked the traveling life, a new town every few days, but not the carney food. Lots of beans, sometimes boiled eggs, and always tough meat. I lived in a small camper with three other guys and with all those beans, you can imagine the smell. We left the windows open most times and suffered the bugs because the smell was so awful. My aspirations were to work up to an Age and Scale man, because they always got the giggling girls. I tried it for a week and didn't have the knack for working the booths, so they assigned me roustie jobs of setting up and taking down the tents. I loaded the same suitcases so much that I can still see them in my sleep. For the little bit of money I made, I felt it was my job to treat carny people's belongings like my own. They were my family, so I handled their stuff with care.

The main problem with the carney is that every night is about making the nut, as if that's the only thing that matters in life. The manager was fair, and took a liking to me as if he was trying to find my place in the show. I never knew much personal about the carney people in our group, except the gossip on the road. Most people liked it that way- they operated under the radar, if you know what I mean. To them, what happened in the past was forgotten and they lived from town to town and tried to do their job. Our outfit avoided the grifters, and ran mostly honest games. By the time we dropped the awnings at any town, I'd learned people were pretty much the same wherever you went, some good, some bad, some stupid, and some cautious. It's funny to me that no matter how bad times were, people managed to find a little money for the carney. It's all different now with video games; the kids spend their money on computer games and not on winning a Kewpie doll for their sweetie.

When winter came and we moved south to Gibtown, there were long stretches without work. Times were hard then. Not as hard as they are now, but hard enough. Folks would not spend their money to win a doll or ride the wheel more than once or twice and even young bucks and their cutie girls looked around more often than they bought. We made some good money on food stands then, but those are different now. We did not have fancy fried candy bars, or fried pickles, just fresh-fried doughnuts with powdered sugar, Pepsi cola, hot dogs, and burgers. The workers got what was thrown out at the end of the night, and anything was better than beans.

I had a few flings with the carney girls. The bearded lady turned out to be one spirited woman. We carried on for some time, till I was distracted by the snake lady. Joanne, the bearded lady, did not take kindly to that distraction and tossed me out. I hear tell she's left the trade, shaved her beard, and works in an office in Ahoskie. I plan to look her up and see if I might be able to fan some smoldering coals. The snake lady was pretty good, but she was into signs. This thing and that thing were always a sign of something. She was always watching those signs; one day, when she saw the sign for me to go, I was out of her camper. The manager was a tough guy, but he had to be to manage that bunch. He had a sharp, barking laugh that didn't quite make it to the corners of his mouth and definitely was never in his eyes. He was good with the customers, especially if he thought they were a ripe mark, and smooth with the local law. His job depended on making the nut just like everyone's did. If we did not make it during a dry spell, someone had to go. One day that was me; they left me around Elberton in Georgia, just across the South Carolina line, with my pay. There were no hard feelings on my side, I miss the people and the travel. After hanging around town for a few days after the carney left, someone asked me if I wanted some work on a farm and I took the job.

I've worked near every kind of pickin' there is and harvesting tobacco is the worst—hot, sweaty, and greasy. In the harvest season the leaves are full of worms, big green tobacco worms that hide under the leaves and jump out at you when you move the leaf. If there were enough worms, someone might spray, because worms damage the leaf. But if the weather won't right, they couldn't spray, and we dealt with the worms. The nastiest kind were large female worms with thousands of little white eggs all over their body. Harvesting tobacco is a touchy business with lots of rows of tobacco, only so much hired help, and always a chance of a bad storm or afternoon lightning. Back when I was working tobacco, a tractor or a horse and cart went down the middle row pulling a wagon. The job is not complicated, just backbreaking. Prime the bottom leaves and set them in the wagon as flat as you could. Those lugs were the lowest value leaves, but they still had to be handled carefully. The foreman was always watching and docked your pay if you damaged leaves. The real money was in the next three layers of leaves; when you were priming those, you needed to pay special attention and set them neat and flat on the trailer so as not to fold or drop the leaves. The tips came last after two to three weeks of work and had very little value, but we picked them just as carefully. In tobacco, there is always someone leaning over your back, telling you to work faster, that you missed something, or were not watching the leaves. Tobacco paid pretty good money. The owners picked us up, dropped us off, and fed us pretty well. During picking time, we worked in the rain and in the sun. When quitting time came, the boss man blew his whistle and we did our counts for the day, loaded onto the truck, and headed for some cool water. I went through a set of clothes a week, and had no way of cleaning them where I was livin, so I had to spend money for washing powder and clean them in the stream next to the house. I pulled corn for a bit, and that might seem easier, but the corn does not want to come off so easy. After pulling a thousand ears, it gets pretty tiring. Most of that hard work is done by machine now. The people who worked the farms are now mostly out of work. I'm glad I'm not doing that outdoor work anymore.

Now I'm here telling you this story and living the easy life in Marsden, getting that social security and welfare and overall doing pretty well.

Patrice

I met Roger at a church dance at the punch bowl. He
stood at the bowl, shifting from one foot to the other,
and it was obvious he had come over to introduce
himself. I was in an upbeat mood, considering I knew
almost no one at a singles dance in a church basement
on a Saturday night. I'd grown bored of sitting at home
while I was getting over James's death and things came
to a head one snowy Sunday evening when I had a
serious talk with myself about the future. Three months
after that, I finally did something and went to the church
dance. I've never been good at meeting people in bars or
on blind dates. In those days, there were not many ways
for single women to meet eligible men except organized
social events.

Over light punch bowl chatter, Roger seemed like a nice
guy—a companion, but not a mate. I guess my emotions
were too frazzled to consider any kind of relationship
just then, but there was something intangible that
signaled that we needed each other. He did not have the
passion or the soul of James, but he had a deep sense of
purpose tempered with vulnerability. There was a
steadiness that appealed to me. I had only a few
relationships to compare; Roger was not James, but

better for me in some deeper way, and that has proven to be true for these twenty-five years of marriage.

I finished college with a teaching degree, then taught for five years, third and fourth grades, in a Catholic school in South Boston. Teaching then was different from teaching now, and I don't regret not keeping up my teaching skills. My life revolved around living in the city, socializing with fellow teachers, and spending weeks in the summer with friends in a rented house close to the Cape. I got more sun than I needed, and burned more often than I should, but loved the ocean air and the freedom of the beach. I met James at the beach and we clicked from the moment we met. With him, I felt that special bond of the first phase of love when everything seems right, conversation is easy, and even the simplest things have a special meaning. It took about a month before I invited him to dinner for my mother to analyze him with her unfailing radar. I was nervous all evening, wanting my parents to like him. After I got home, I called her to find out the verdict. "He's nice" was her only comment. Of course I wanted a lot more detail, but that was mom. She added, "Your father likes him and thinks he has potential." Hardly an overwhelming endorsement I guess, but a positive one I could build on. I worked it as any marriageable woman works it with more parent visits in different situations to increase their comfort level with James. It was all fitting together.

We spent most of our time together and two years passed quickly. My parents were still their strict selves and cautioned me about seeing him too much, but I only half listened to them. After all, I was twenty years old and out of their house. Fate intervened before James and I had to make any serious decisions. On our second anniversary of dating, James drove home from dinner at the house and was killed by a drunk driver. A head-on collision, the police said, that killed him instantly. It took until morning for me to learn of his death on the news. My name and contact information were not in his wallet, and so I heard the news like every other person in Boston. Our plans and our lives were shattered in that instant and I withdrew into myself. Of course the shock lessened with time and reality started to set in. I cried nightly for two things: our lost life together and having to start over again in a dating world that was foreign.

Then I met Roger at the punch bowl. I'd had one half-hearted series of three dates, and I told Roger about him and about the time with James. I believed in full disclosure and listed all my relationships for Roger when he proposed. Strangely, he never told me about old girlfriends or what had become of them. Maybe he never had any or maybe he was forgetting some unpleasantness.

Our relationship progressed in the usual way, with cups of coffee on lunch breaks at school. He came there and would wait quietly in the teachers' lounge for me to finish class and talk with wayward students. After a time, I introduced him to co-workers and we progressed to home cooked dinners, first at my house and then, after a time, at his. I would occasionally stay the night. After a year, a certainty dawned on me, rich and absolutely believable, that a part of my life had ended and something new had begun: at a primal level, I knew, I knew Roger was the one I would grow old with. By taking his hand, a simple gesture, I put all of my baggage aside and embraced his nourishment of our future. I have been mostly happy with my choice of Roger as a mate, because he's good for me in a way James would not have been.

My family was in the demographic of middle class. In the 1950s middle class meant well-off compared with our neighbors. I am an only child and a product of my mother's overwhelming influence. She was a self-made woman before that term became popular, and often reminded me that I needed to start flying right, along her path, if I wanted to make anything of myself. Lest I forget my heritage and her grit, she used phrases like

> "When you're faced with real troubles, you won't be able to sit back and think about it, you'll have to act and act quickly."

> "You have to be on your guard all the time because evil can be as close as your backyard or as the person next to you in the movie theater."

"Bad people would just love to get hold of a young girl like you. They might be standing peacefully next to you one minute, and then jab a needle of drugs into your shoulder the next and haul you away. How would you get out of that fix?"

As you might expect, in her household I was constantly alert and suspicious as if I some unseen evil force might jump out from a dark alley and whisk me away. While her cautions are necessary in today's world, they were over the top in those simpler times.

My mother, Marta, became self-made at sixteen. She left an unhappy home to find more in the world than small town New England could offer. She secured a position as a governess for a Lutheran minister and his family who were moving to Egypt. That was in 1937, and his calling was to minister to the natives of Egypt, a British protectorate then. Reverend Proctor was an upstanding man and his wife and three children lived the quiet life of a minister's family in conservative New England. Mother knew little of their lives in the states before she took the governess position, but heard about it in great detail later from Mrs. Camilla Proctor on many occasions. Mom interviewed with them in Boston at a coffee shop. She saw photos of the three children and heard how bright the eldest girl was, how athletic the two boys were—angels all. Mom must have impressed them, because they hired her on the spot. They told her of their plans to move to Egypt in a month and asked if she would be able to get her affairs in order. What affairs she had were not a problem; she had left home just a few days before and carried all her belongings in a small suitcase. They offered for her to stay in the guest room of their home until the sailing date. Mom did not feel it was necessary to inform her family of this adventure, as her leaving had been unpleasant. Staying at their home would allow her to meet the children in their home and prepare to tutor them in routine subjects on the ship. Mrs. Proctor felt that the long ocean crossing would give them all time to get to know each other. Governess duties were to be some schooling on the crossing and light housework and cooking when they arrived in Egypt. That suited Mom just fine, and the pay of sixty dollars a month was more than generous with essentially all expenses paid. It was not a problem that she had only gone to high school for a few years. She had been a bright student and projected a good image.

As you would expect, she told me many stories of this period in her life, and all were interwoven with the caution, uncertainty and adventure of moving to a foreign country. She gave examples of the joy of the Proctor household and the exceptional abilities of the children in academics and sports. Time passed and Egypt became more aware of the coming Nazi influence in the world. The family was caught in the war and unable to leave Egypt until 1940 when they escaped to London in a clandestine retreat from advancing German forces, crossing borders at night with a guidee. Their passage to London was in a cargo ship in steerage class with the family all huddled together below decks with little food and less sanitation. One of the children died on the passage from a spread of diphtheria in steerage and was buried at sea.

In London, the family was broke and broken. Reverend Proctor was eventually able to convince the Lutheran synod to provide a loan and a job in a small church on the outskirts of London. War followed them to London with bombings and the blitz. One of Mom's favorite stories was of being blown off an outhouse toilet by a rocket blast in the neighborhood. Most indoor plumbing was destroyed by bombing. The only facilities were portable outhouses, two for each street, provided by the government, but emptied by the residents when overflowing.

Marta, now battle tested, made it through the war and came back to Boston. She married my father, an electrician, who had just finished technical school after returning from the war. The shortage of men limited her choice in mates. My father was a quiet man, a polar opposite from Marta. She never contacted her family again and never heard from the Proctors again. She believed in cutting ties and leaving them cut.

My childhood was happy and I progressed as a child without incident, but always aware of my mothers' cautions, because I heard them almost daily. I was thin and incredibly flexible. I loved to stand and twist my arms and legs into impossible positions. Relaxing meant turning my right hip inward and pulling my right foot around the leg into an impossible angle. People looked at me as if I should be in pain, but I was as relaxed and comfortable as in any other position, and perhaps more so.

When I was in high school, I needed a job to save money for college. My family had done business with the local drug store and I approached Mr. Wiley Oakley, the owner, for a part time position. I had an interest in pharmacy dispensing, and wanted to try it out before majoring in science and pharmacy in college. Mr. Oakley would not allow me to handle medications, perhaps suspicious of young people in the 1960s, and gave me a job as a soda fountain worker. Boston was a series of self-contained neighborhoods, and his was a popular neighborhood store; a combination hangout, convenience store, and lunch counter. Regulars came to the soda fountain for lunch, and we did a brisk business the six days it was open with lunch and kids coming in for soda and shakes after school. I was one of two people behind the counter during busy times, the other was the head person (Debie). I was a replacement for the popular Sybil. Sybile was on medical leave recovering from having her gallbladder removed and had to stay off her feet for three months. Her illness and recovery was perfect timing for me as I only had three months before I started college. The hours were 8:00 a.m. to 5:00 p.m. and the products were simple: flavored cokes, Sundaes, cones, and floats. There were a lot of variations from what people had gotten used to from Sybil: making shakes thick or thin, cokes heavily or lightly flavored, mixed flavors, and different toppings. It wasn't so much complicated as it was finding out who liked what. Syble always remembered each customer and their preferences. Some customers seemed peeved that they had to tell me what they wanted. I gained about fifteen pounds that summer because I never got the combination of ice cream and milk right and there were always a few sips left in the bottom of the shake mixer. Rather than letting it go to waste, I drank it. Mr. Oakley let us eat whatever we wanted for lunch, so I almost always had a burger and fries and maybe a leftover hot dog before I went off shift. My specialty became the strawberry shake with three scoops of dipped strawberry ice cream, whole milk, some strawberry syrup (unless it was William Riley who wanted chocolate syrup), and whirl it until it got to the correct thickness. My special touch was a swirl of strawberry syrup on the top before I put on the whipped cream. Sundaes were easier because we only offered limited choices, chocolate nut and a banana split. We did not have a heater for hot fudge and nobody wanted caramel sundaes in those days. Splits were the old fashioned kind with a whole banana, scoops of vanilla, chocolate, and strawberry ice cream as well as toppings that matched like: marshmallow as the vanilla topping except if you were Rhonda Sparks who wanted the toppings to be shifted so the chocolate was on the vanilla ice cream and so on. She always wanted two cherries on the top and a lot of whipped cream, but she was a big girl anyway. Some wanted pineapple toppings, some wanted wet nuts and some wanted dry nuts, but everyone wanted whipped cream and a cherry. I couldn't resist taking an extra cherry as I made the sundae.

Debie, my supervisor, (one B, IE and a heart drawn over the letter I) was in charge of the grill and cooked all the burgers and fries. Her specialty was fries with a scoop of beef gravy smeared over the top. Debie put so much gravy on the plate that you couldn't use your fingers. You just can't get gravy fries in the South.

After working the fountain, I'd clean the six tables and reset them with silverware and napkins as well as refill water. Men would joke with me, flirting at the counter but not at the tables for some reason. Maybe they didn't want their friends to see their flirting technique? I smiled politely, but Mom's influence made me wary of strangers.

New love is every girl's dream and I wondered when my prince would come. Love was different in the 1960s, different than in any other decade, and perhaps that's because I met my first love on January 2, 1960.

I think of him as a suitor; he would be called a lover nowadays. I was seventeen and he was the first man my parents allowed me to date. I was enthralled by the attentions of an accomplished man. He devoted himself to winning a part of me, and it was easy for him to enchant me and enchantment quickly led to surrender. Before he tired of me and my naiveté, he gave me a scarf as a present. In his room, before we went out to dinner, he handed me the box. When I opened it and unfolded the paper, I gently lifted the teal scarf. He had me wrap it around my neck and drape it against my bare skin. He smiled, pleased with his choice of color, because it enhanced the color of my eyes and blended well with my skin tones. On our times out that winter, I would always wear the scarf and coordinated my outfits around it. My mother laughed that I would wear it out, and suspected there was more to the gift than I was telling her. The other day I came across that scarf in a drawer and when I put it on, the memories of him and that time came flooding back as if it were yesterday. I spent more time than I should have studying the scarf and my eyes in the mirror to see if his compliment was still valid. After I'd answered that question to my satisfaction, the scarf went back in the drawer and I went back to rolling Roger's socks and folding his underwear, because he likes them to be in order in his drawer.

Roger relies on Met for his news about Marsden, but my friend and local advisor is Lizbeth, Lizzie to most everyone. She is a crusty, well-proportioned middle-aged woman, equally friendly, pragmatic, and distrustful. She is a keen judge of character with a deep personal strength honed on years of dealing with the public in the South. She has a wide, toothy smile that people remember. Marsden people find it an odd friendship between us and wonder what we could possibly have in common. Surprisingly, we have similar views, born from different cultures. Lizzie adds the perspective of life for a black woman raised in Marsden during a time of social upheaval in the South. We connected at a Saturday morning farmer's market, before the market moved downtown, when it was still close to the credit union. Back then, it was a pretty lonely market, even in the summer, and only a few farm families brought their produce into town for sale. I love fresh produce and Lizzie was working at her family's stand. I was feeling a ripe tomato, and it rolled out of my hand and onto the ground. I picked it up and placed it back on the pile. Lizzie smiled and asked whether I wanted that tomato in a bag, or to carry it home. There was no doubt of the message—you dropped it, you bought it. I do not easily blush but did then. Since that day, I've enjoyed a special link with Lizzie, regularly meeting for lunch at the house or downtown for girl chat. Lizzie has an endless knowledge of things Marsden and we are the yin and yang of life with two views on any topic, one local and one Yankee. She prefers Lizzie to the more formal Lizbeth, or as she puts it, "Lizzie is my real name for friends; Lizbeth is my legal name for getting married or divorced." Lizzie has an opinion on any subject, usually based on a blend of local lore, family tradition, and religious principles.

Lizzie

We grew up poor; but the funny thing was that no-one ever told us we were poor, so we didn't act poor. I was born to a young mother who was not married and raised by my grandparents. When I was about a year old, my momma and daddy got married, but I continued to live with my grandparents.

I grew up just south of Marsden and all of my people were sharecroppers. At that time the arrangement was that sharecroppers were paid a bit for working tobacco and cucumbers, but not for other crops since we harvested those for free. We lived in a house on the land as part of our pay. My extended family of aunts, uncles, and cousins all worked the fields so that we could have enough money to get through the year. Even with all those workers, most years we weren't able to earn enough to make it through the long dry spell till cash crops came back. Each year my grandpop had to go to the owner and borrow fifty dollars, sometimes more, against the next season's profits for us to make it through the year. I know that today fifty dollars doesn't sound like much, but a dollar bought a lot back then. My grandparents carefully spent that money for food we couldn't grow and occasionally for clothes. This was in the 50s. My family worked the Tucker farm.

I was the only girl for a while, and my grandparents sheltered me. I was considered ugly as a child and lots of folks, even family, would talk about how ugly I was in those quiet tones children always overhear from adults. I guess that as I grew up most of that ugliness passed out of me. I went to the First-Third Marsden Training school, a school for black children in that area. Most of the kids in the class were my relatives because my family had lived in the area for a long time. In that school, we had the same teacher year after year, so the teacher got to know each boy or girl well—the good ones and the troublemakers. The teacher for most of my time there, Mr. Lafayette Williams, expected us to perform well in class. This meant doing all our homework, and being able to recite the lesson when we were called to the chalkboard. About once a week some kid, usually a boy, had not done his work at home and it showed when Mr. Williams called him to the chalkboard. After a few minutes of embarrassing the person with his silent anger, Mr. Williams would unexpectedly give them a whollop on the soft back part of their legs with his giant hand. He was a big man and that whollop nearly lifted the person off their feet. I'm not saying I never had any whollops, but I saw enough of them to remember them well. Funny thing was that he didn't always whollop the person; so you couldn't flinch and protect yourself, he made it a surprise.

We couldn't afford to go to the doctor if we got sick. Grandmomma was an expert at home remedies and used several of them at once to beat back even a few sniffles. I remember getting really sick when I was about eight and coughing a lot with shaking fevers. Grandmomma took me into the city to Dr. Haar's office because her remedies were not working. There was a black man who ran the elevator up to the third floor. I remember him looking at me as we rode up like he was pretty sure I was too sick to come up. He looked worried that if I went up, I might not come back down standing, but in a hospital bed or worse. In the doctor's office there was a white waiting room and a colored waiting room across the hall from each other. To me it seemed no colored people were attended to, no matter how sick they were, until all the white people had been seen. Maybe that was true and maybe it was just my imagination. We got back to see the doctor close to the end of the afternoon. I'd been coughing in the waiting room for most of the afternoon and my chest hurt. Dr. Haar treated me kindly and smiled as he listened to my chest, even when I had to cough. After he finished listening to me, and took that cold stethoscope off my chest, he told my grandmomma very quietly that I had a very bad case of pneumonia. He reached up high on a shelf and poured some white pills into a paper napkin and told her to give them to me four times a day. He did not ask us to come back for a follow up, and I always wondered about that. If I was so sick, why did he not want to see if his medicine worked? The cost for the visit and the medicine was ten dollars, almost a quarter of what my grandpa had to borrow for us to get through that season. I was embarrassed that I had cost my family so much money, but everyone seemed to be glad when I got better. I never saw another doctor until I delivered my children.

About this time, my momma and daddy left to sharecrop on another farm. I had a brother and sister by this time, and they went with my momma, but I stayed with my grandparents. I told people that I was lucky enough to have two daddies and two mommas. That was probably a common thing to say, but I thought of myself as lucky.

We had no money for toys, so we made toys from things around the yard. I made a pusher from a lid and a broken tobacco stick and pushed dirt, stones, and most anything else around the dusty yard for hours at a time. When I was about ten, we got some marbles and jacks. I loved hopscotch or jump rope in the dust around the house. We didn't do that fancy double-dutch the girls do nowadays; we just jumped in and kept the rhythm.

In the fall my family got together with neighbors for a hog killin'. We'd raised those hogs all year and now it was their time. In the cooler weather in fall, the meat would hold over better. Fall still brings back memories of the smells of bacon, ham and sausage. All the families around us killed their hogs about the same time, so my people were always going to a hog killin' on a weekend. If it was busy and the weather had been bad, sometimes people got together after a day of work. It got darker earlier of course, so the best time for the killin' was early on a Saturday morning. Usually four or five families brought their hogs because once the process got set up and the people knew what they were to do, the work went quickly. My grandmomma joked that she could cook everything in the hog except the squill.

When I was about eleven, the Marsden Training School was integrated with a nearby white school. Integration was a big deal in Eastern North Carolina, but I don't recall fights between black and white kids, although I heard there were plenty after school among the older kids. Not much changed for me with integration; I still worked hard in school. One thing that did change. There was no wholloping by any teacher. Looking back on it, a good stiff smack on the back of your legs seemed to serve a purpose because when it stopped, kids backslid. When there was nothing to stop contrary behavior, kids continued backsliding and eventually stopped coming to school altogether. I knew I'd find a personal wholloping at home if my grandmomma heard that I was not doing what I was supposed to do in school. She kept me on a pretty tight leash and busy with field work, chores, homework, church, and a little time for play.

Around us there was a local BBQ place with the pig cooked over an open pit in the back. It was a white restaurant, and no colored people could go inside to get food, but they could order at the back door. One Friday afternoon I went with my granddaddy to get some BBQ. He knocked on the back door and a big white man came out and growled, 'Watcha wont'. My granddaddy told him he wanted some BBQ and rib bones. The man brought the meat wrapped up in some newspaper. I recall the wonderful smell on the long walk home, but my grandpop did not open the package to sneak a taste. At Christmas time, the owner of the farm we were cropping on gave our family a big platter of BBQ from this same restaurant to thank us for the work we had done over the year.

I loved Christmas time with my family; Grandmomma would save a bit of money all year long and buy fruits like apples, oranges, and those nasty grapes with big seeds. She kept the fruit under her bed, but we knew where she hid them by the fine smell coming from that room. We were forbidden to touch any of these treats until Christmas Eve, when she would let us each pick one fruit. When I was about eight, I got a special present for Christmas—a white doll baby. Maybe there were black doll babies, but my doll baby had been in another family, and I got her used. Having that doll baby made me feel more like a girl than anything else up to then.

My worst memory of those times was from a summer night when I was about six years old. I was spending the night with my aunt and uncle about five miles from home. In the middle of the night, a bright light woke me up and I looked out to see a cross burning in the front yard. There were about fourteen people standing around the cross holding long firesticks. They were wearing white robes and pointed white hoods with holes where their eyes and mouth would be. It was a perfectly quiet night with no crickets or any animal sounds, just the burning wood crackling. None of the people in the yard made a sound; they just turned their heads to look from the cross to our house. They must have seen us looking out the windows. Right away, my uncle turned off the lights and told us to keep our heads away from the windows and to make no noises. He told us that if we were quiet, these people would go away. After about an hour, the light from the cross got dimmer and the people slowly walked off down the road. I still remember the cross, the smell of burning wood and the whiteness of their robes. No-one else I ever knew had a meeting with Klan folks, but the sharpness of that memory stays with me even today.

I remember how special it was when my granddaddy got a TV. It was one of those old round ones with the small screen and big furniture cabinet. He got it used from someone. We only got channel nine and it was usually more sound than picture. Still, seeing a picture, even a fuzzy one, was so much better than radio. The Marsden newspaper at the time had a special column in the weekend edition called *Colored Folks News*. No colored person I ever heard wrote it, so it must have been written by white people because it had news that didn't seem to matter to my family. Down the road, there was a drive-in called the Plitt that we went to for a special treat. To tell the truth, I cannot remember a single movie at that drive-in. It was some time before my friends had a car to get us there. Usually for fun I'd stand in front of the train depot on a sunny Saturday afternoon and nobody cared if I hung around as long as I did not bother anyone. I wondered where on Earth all these people were going and feared they might not know their way home to their people. I thought they might just wander around lost in the vast world outside of Eastern North Carolina.

Things changed for me in eleventh grade. Boys started to notice me. I was surprised at the attention, because they did not think I was as ugly as my family had always told me. Back then the boys wore a lot of grease in their hair. I've always thought that for a boy to have comb marks in his hair marked him as trashy. I met my first husband at school. He was in the Army and came to one of our dances when he was home. Up till then, my grandmomma would not hear of boys coming by or paying me any attention. She liked him though. He was kind, bought me things, and we sparked along pretty quickly. I got married in that eleventh grade year and during my senior year had our first child. Because he was in the service, he was stationed in Richmond. When my son was born, Grandma made it clear that I was going to finish school. She would care for him during the day; but when that bus let me off and my feet hit the ground, he was mine. In the summer I worked in the fields to save money for our family, saving that money plus some my husband sent back gave us more savings than we'd ever had in our lives. It was sad moving out and leaving my family, but my husband, my son, and I moved with the military.

As you can tell from that story, I've seen things change in Eastern North Carolina—some have even changed for the better. My opinions come from my life lived on the land and from meeting good people and bad people. I think my greatest talent is to be able to tell the difference.

Stories from Marsden

Lizzie's friend Shirleen

Love mysteriously finds its way, ignoring personalities and human frailties to settle on a balance point and shifting over the life of a relationship to meet the needs of a couple. Jimmy is in love with his wife Shirleen, and she once loved Jimmy. He has one talent that holds the relationship together: he is an extraordinary fisherman.

In Marsden, fishing on the river is a combination of luck and skill, although it's uncertain about how much is luck and how much is skill. Jimmy is a legend because of his skill, and folks watch closely when he comes to fish in order to learn his secrets. It is rumored that he can tune his mind to read the water; and drop his line where the fish will bite. When he settles on a fishing spot, he stands tall and still with his body leaned out toward the river and looks just below the surface to feel the power of the water, then drops his line. His choice of bait is not important, but he prefers a flounder rig and live minnows to artificial bait. No matter what he uses, in fewer than five casts he will have a legal fish. Flounder is his specialty because it's Shirleen's favorite.

"I don't live at home," says Jimmy, holding back the most interesting parts of the story. "Me and Shirleen can't live in the same house, but mostly it's Shirleen that has a problem with me staying. She doesn't take well to my going off fishing with my buddies. Those trips have gotten me in trouble a few times. Funny thing about it is that she loves the fish but has her own thoughts about what else might go on during those trips besides fishing. All of that is mostly her imagination. Sure, there were times when we'd be drinking and playing cards and maybe some women might come over, but I never did anything. Shirleen is just the suspicious type. In the last six months, she's softened a bit, and will let me come home for the night if I bring some fish. Without the fish, forget any visits." If the fish have been biting, Jimmy rides his bike to the house and knocks with the freshly cleaned fish on a stringer and a smile on his face.

"I know how he is about his fishing and no matter what else you say about Jimmy, that man can fish," Shirleen says as she cocks her head from under her sun hat. "There's an evil side to him, and he's hurt me in most all the ways that a woman can be hurt. Hurt is one thing, but my weakness is fresh fish. When that man shows up with flounder, I can set aside our disagreement for just that night. I don't forget any of the past; I'll never forget. There's a world of difference between setting aside and forgetting."

"When I knock on Shirleen's door, I never know if things are going to work out. I've had her slam the door in my face if the fish were not to her liking. If luck is with me, and if it's been awhile since my last visit, and if she likes the look of the fish, she'll smile her special smile and invite me in. I know it sounds silly, but walking into my own house holding a stringer of fish can be a moving experience…because I know what's coming later. I've learned to wait in the parlor while she takes the fish to the kitchen. There she'll be making up a special batter and resting the fish in it while she heats the frying oil."

"Just because he's in the door doesn't mean he can start his old ways, so I make him sit away from me in the parlor to make it clear that he's here because of the fish, only because of the fish, and not because of any closeness between us. I use cast iron for the frying because it holds heat better. If the temperature's right, each piece only takes a few minutes. I love the spark and sizzle of battered fish hitting hot oil. My momma taught me that if it's all right with the oil, when that fish floats to the top, he's done just right. If I'm in a good mood I wonder what Jimmy's thinking about out there and whether he's sorry for his ways. Realistically, I know what he's thinking. I'll let him hold those thoughts to himself for a while. He's made me hold enough anxieties waiting for him to come back from a fishing trip, knowing from my friends before he ever came up the steps what he and his buddies had been up to."

"I know what she's doing in the kitchen and cooking is only a part of it. She's going over every bad thing I ever did to her and deciding if the fish is worth it. On the plus side, I've never had her throw me out once she saw the fish, but she's made my collar rub plenty rough while I wait for her. I think times with Shirleen may be better because those running times are done. I'm getting too old and most of the guys have settled down, so going out of town on a wild fishing trip just doesn't happen any more. The last time we went, it was easy to find the cards and the beer but harder to find any women. They all seem to like younger men or men with money."

Shirleen likes to do her frying on the porch off the kitchen so the fish smell does not linger around in the morning. In Shirleen's mind, fried fish and Jimmy are best enjoyed in short spells with no holdover memories.

"When I smell that smell from the plate of golden brown fish, I can't hold out any longer and I come to the table and nod for him to come over. He knows to sit quietly at the table. If I want to talk, I'll ask him something; otherwise, he's there to watch me eat fish. I'm embarrassed that fish has that hold over me, but as I eat each piece the tastes of the breading and the freshness of the fish is almost sinful. I'm pretty sure the Reverend won't be preaching about that sin though, so I can enjoy it without feeling guilty. Some nights I feel generous and save him the last piece.—most nights, not."

"It pains me to watch those fish come off that plate so fast, because I know none are coming my way. I feel the smell in my nose and the flavor on my tongue, but it goes no further. After the last piece, she leans back, sighs, and licks her lower lip as if to recall the flavor of that last bite. As she leaves the table, I hope the mood is right. I've found it's lucky for me to get over to my old recliner and wait while she clears and straightens. When things suit her, she sniffs the air one last time and strolls back to the bedroom. I watch her walk down the hallway and get an image of the fire just under the surface waiting to be released."

"Men are so predictable. I know what he's here for and what he's been thinking. I used to be torn between gratefulness for him bringing the fish and my recall of his cheating ways. Now both of those emotions have taken a back seat, and I can think about what I want. After the fish are gone, most nights I walk down the hall, turn just so, and look in Jimmy's direction. He follows as if I'd flipped his leash." In the morning, Shirleen is up early and out to visit her friends. The unspoken rule is that Jimmy leaves things as they were and is gone by the time she gets back.

Things were as good as both lovers needed them until a few weeks ago. Jimmy got the boys together for an out of town trip to bring back old times, times full of all the reasons they went out of town. A week after he got home, his fishing hit a string of bad luck. "I can't catch a thing, no matter where I go or what I'm using," he says with that tired look of a fishing man come on tough times. People shake their heads at his lost talent. They watch him stand on the shore for hours with an empty hook, knowing that his bait is gone but not even motivated enough to re-bait the hook. He can't read the water or the fish. The truth is that he needs some fish ... and a visit to Shirleen.

Jimmy scratched his chin as he reflected on the loss of his skill. "I've thought about it a lot and something's changed in my mind. I can't read the fish like I used to. Earl thinks Shirleen had a hex placed on my fishing pole. She has a friend who knows how to set a hex, and I believe she paid her a visit after this last fishing trip. The fishing trip was fantastic, just like the old days. Earl and the rest of the guys laughed about how young we felt, breaking loose without that noose around our necks. As usual, Earl started the party after fishing by opening a jug of his homemade liquor. Things progressed from there. The women came over about midnight and the party got considerably cozier. I suspect that Shirleen found out the details from one of her gossipy friends and that was the end of her patience. She's the kind of woman who will hit where it hurts most, and I'll bet she took it out on my fishing."

Shirleen was downtown telling the story to her friend. "It does my heart good to know that he can't fish after that hex took hold. When I came crying to my auntie after his last trip, she suggested teaching him a lesson and pointed me to a woman who knows about placing hexes. That woman had a creepy air about her, but I heard she did good work. All she needed for the job was something he loved, and it was easy to borrow his favorite fishing pole for a few hours. Setting a solid hex on something is powerful punishment and removing it is nearly impossible. Now that it's done, I hear fishing for Jimmy is a frustrating time, as it should be. With the market just down the street, I can do without Jimmy's fish and without his foolishness. The market fish aren't as fresh, but they satisfy me just fine and there are no strings attached. Besides, the man behind the counter has gotten real friendly lately."

"It took me some thought to figure out about the hex," Jimmy says as he tells the story. "The more I thought about it, the more it made sense. I consulted with Earl when he wasn't drunk, because those are the times when he's the most helpful. He told me about a woman he knew a few miles north of town who could lift a hex. According to him, she had a powerful gift and worked cheap. Earl smiled his sneaky smile and warned me to be on my guard because this woman was a witch and played as many dirty tricks as she placed spells.

I found her at the dark end of a long dirt road. Her two room shack stood on a wood foundation so rotted that a good wind might bring everything down. I knocked and the door creaked open as if pulled inward by a sprit. The crinkled newsprint on the walls in the front room was glued to the boards from floor to ceiling, the print arranged in whatever direction pleased her. Faded news photos of smiling people stared back into the room as they watched over her, an audience whenever she wanted one. The woman rocking in the chair was past old and past thin, a bony shroud barely moving the rocker. The gray skin of her cheeks and temples stretched tight across bone was a contrast to bright black eyes glowing out of her skull. Her hair was the thinnest of threads and arranged in some random manner, like trying to hold dust in place. The color of everything in the room was a combination of gray light and brown dirt. As I waited in front of the open door, she looked up at me from her chair and her glowing eyes scared me."

Jimmy shivered when he recalled the cool breeze that pulled him over the threshold. The door creaked closed behind him as the woman sized him up. She stared for a minute or so, then croaked for him to speak up or leave, mumbling like she had a mouthful of chew. Jimmy gathered enough courage to get out his question about removing hexes. Her toothless mouth curled into a lopsided smile as she nodded and spit a wad of tobacco juice toward a hole in the middle of the floor. Most missed the hole and splattered onto his shoe. The remaining stray brown drops dribbled down the corner of her mouth. Jimmy was afraid in that room, afraid of the evil he never knew circulated among the living.

She swiped her mouth on her sleeve and nodded for him to tell his story. Out came the details about Shirleen and the fishing pole, and he rushed to let her know he wanted the hex removed. He spared the details of why Shirleen had the hex placed. Her eyes bored into him as she listened and wandered over the pictures on the wall as she thought, silently consulting the people in the photos. Then she coughed from somewhere deep in her chest and spoke. Her voice sounded like the chew and the liquid were still playing around in her mouth, mumbling, "Spells hold tight if you place them right, and a tight spell is nearly impossible to remove. I hope you know that the hex is on you, and the pole is just the resting place for the spell. Maybe I can try to weaken it. You need to know that I've had times where I messed with a hard-set spell and sunk it in deeper, more powerful. My work may not help in the way you want it to, and I might need several tries to get it right. Even then, I may only be able to weaken the power a little. Do you have money?"

"I handed over all the money I had, two twenty-dollar bills. She snatched the bills from my hand, ran her fingers over them, and stuffed them into some fold deep in her shawl."

"Show me the pole." He passed it over to her and she laid it in the middle of the floor. She crouched over it, eyes closed and legs spread, feeling the power of the spell. Then she moved in a circle around the pole, crabbing across the floor, around and around. She knelt and ran her fingers up and down on the pole, working hard on the handle and not touching the reel, lids fluttering and mumbling words he did not understand. Suddenly, she stood and handed him the pole. "Try that," she mumbled through her toothless smile, and with a glance at the photos on the wall, spit a final time and walked through a curtain into a back room and disappeared.

As Jimmy told Earl later, "I was too shocked to ask for some money back. She had not done much work for that forty dollars, but her attitude seemed final and I sure didn't want to leave her angry. As I started down the steps, I heard her cackling and mumbling. I wish I could say things were back to normal, but they're not. The pole was some better for the week after I visited her and I caught a few fish, but I could tell my mind was still not tuned with the fish. I borrowed a pole from Earl, but caught nothing. I've got a mind to go back there and demand that she take another try to remove the hex, and I'll be taking Earl with me. Maybe her laugh was because of some trick and she drove the spell deeper. Maybe I can convince Shirleen to lift the hex if I promise never to go off with the boys again. I'm getting too old for their partying anyway. If I can get that far, Shirleen might go back to her woman and lighten the hex and I can be back in the fishing business."

"That Jimmy just never quits," Shirleen laughed. "He must be hurting pretty bad because he's started coming over for the last week with cheap gifts, barbeque, some glass beads, and a scarf from somewhere. He even tried some romantic talk, and I laughed inside at his plan to get me to remove the hex. Auntie says that sometimes if the person admits placing a hex and forgives, it can come off. For Jimmy, I may admit to placing it, but there will be no forgiveness. I enjoy seeing him squirm, but a part of me misses the fish."

Now that he can't catch a fish to save his soul, he has to get them in creative ways. When he is doing odd jobs for people at the river, Jimmy casually asks for fish from anyone having some luck from the shore. Even though nobody knows the ins and outs of the story, some people may have kindly feelings and he sometimes gets some fish. Four legal fish used to be the entry ticket to see Shirleen, but if one was a good-sized flounder, she might let him in with three. Maybe he can find a way to talk about that hex the next time she lets him in.

Back at the cabin, the witch croaked a laugh as she talked to the skinny black cat beside her chair. "People are so stupid. One comes to place a hex and pays me good, then another comes to get the hex removed and pays me not as good. I do my best work for the person with the most money."

Lizzie discusses Southern men

Some time after Roger and I moved to Marsden, Lizzie and I got together on a sunny spring morning for a girl chat. Just below our window a group of mallards were mating in the yard and the show set the mood for our talk. I wanted to learn more about Lizzie, nosy I guess. We'd been casual friends for months, but I didn't know a thing about her personal life. She'd helped me with the new customs of living in Marsden, and I wanted to return the favor. I was mostly curious about her impressions of Southern men and her past relationships. She is a witty woman and this topic might give us both a laugh with her keen observations. With the mallards squalling in the background, I asked, "Lizzie, what are your thoughts on Southern men?"

She leaned back in the chair and smiled. Maybe she was deciding how much to share as she scooched forward in a kind of conspiratorial pose and started her story.

"Patsy, a year or so after my husband Lester left, I started to feel more and more that I needed a man. Not for the usual things, at least right now, but for the little things about a man that can be irritating or charming depending on the situation. Mostly I missed giving a man the three C's of Southern hospitality: cookin', cleanin', and carin' for. For the Southern men I've known, the carin' for is especially satisfying and gets the most appreciation. Most of my men I knew took to it like a dog scratched behind his ears.

Men have always been attracted to me, not crazy-attracted mind you, but enough to show me considerable attention. Maybe it's because I'm independent. I don't dress for men. I stopped that nonsense years ago when I realized that men have a closed mind when it comes to the finer points of women's clothing. It's hard to get dressing just right with a man. If you go high brow he gets turned off because you're uppity; if you go low brow, then he reads it as a loose woman looking for something. I found the best way is to dress how you want and then it's his problem to figure it out.

I don't dislike men; they're fine as far as it goes and for what they do well. I can't abide their shenanigans and sooner or later they all seem to have some kind of shenanigans. My first, Lester, was mostly a good husband, but he had about equal amounts of good and evil running through his body. Eventually the evil won out and he started catting around. Marsden is so small that everyone knew it. When it got bad, my friends finally told me. After I did some checking, I shut him out and changed the locks. He was gone to me when those locks got changed.

After Lester, I took up with Earnest, partly for companionship and partly because he stirred my blood. We progressed pretty fast and after a few dates he wanted to move into my house; said he loved me and could not stand to be away from me. My blood was still hot at that point so I took him in. For a few weeks it was like a honeymoon. He was good and did things around the house to help, and I cooked his favorites. The rest was marvelous.

After a few months he started being quiet-like and looking out the window a lot, looking for something or somebody, but he would never say what. I asked him to talk to me so I could help with whatever was bothering him, but he got quiet and more jumpy, especially at night. Most nights he woke up with bad dreams after tossing around in bed and then left the bedroom. He sat in the chair in the front room all night, staring at nothing on the TV.

One morning I came into the front room and saw him sitting in a chair on the back porch. That seemed unusual. When I went out to check on him, he was tied to the chair and had a bullet hole in the side of his head with just one trickle of blood clotted on his cheek. Seeing something like that changes a person forever."

After a pause she walked over to the window and looked out over the water for a time. She twisted her hands as if working something out. When she turned back, there were tears in her eyes.

"I don't know why I told you that because no-one else knows the whole story. Thank you for letting me tell it in my own way. It feels better to get the story told."

She continued, the words tumbling out as her hands twisted with the tension.

"Losing Earnest so suddenly caused me deeper pain than when I tossed Lester out. For me the sharpest pain was around the familiar things like his smell, his smile, and his eyes. It took a powerful effort for me to forget those familiar things. For a time I hated God for what he'd taken from me. When I cried, I searched for any prayer that might ease my pain and pulled it into my mind. I felt helpless talking to a God who did only as pleased him.

Luckily the mind heals over time. Forgetting came on its own and blurry old images slipped away as fresh ones replaced them. Every image that left made Earnest less a part of my life, until finally only a nugget stayed. Some things I can never forget have stayed even to today, but those memories don't have any emotion. I guess that's the sign of healing, and maybe that's God's work.

Not many people get a second chance in love. That first time is a magic time of innocence. Lester and I had it, and then it was gone. Loving after that first time is guarded and protective. I don't think men ever change much. They're either mostly bad or mostly good; if you decide to love them, you have to accept the bad or the good until they give you cause to get rid of them. I believe that women have a curse on them since Eve ate the apple: we're always looking for second chances. We mostly end up making the same bad choice we made the first time, and that's the curse.

This part of the story is about Colerain and how I met him. It all started with him paying me attention last spring on a Saturday morning. He's a classy man, dresses well, and has none of those comb tracks in greasy hair that some men feel is a sign of money. When he smiles, it's a genuine smile, but inside that smile is a man with mischief about him waiting to rain it down on some poor soul. I guess the way I took to his attention and what it might mean for the future is complicated.

I'd moved into a new house on East Second and needed to decorate. All my old stuff went out the door when that sorry so-and-so Bobby left me with his debts and a house full of messy furniture with grease spots where he'd laid his head down. I haven't told you about Bobby yet and will maybe another time when my anger goes down a bit. On that Saturday morning I was hanging out at garage sales looking to buy some OPS (other-people's stuff) to furnish my new place.

In the springtime folks seem to want to trade up to better stuff. The Missus gets tired of the clutter collected over the cold months and calls a yard sale. It was 6:15 a.m.on Saturday, early enough for me to be first in line for prime furniture, but not so early to be seen as a stalker.

The yard sale folks had moved the heavy pieces out the night before, and I'd ridden by a few times and saw the couch and chairs I wanted. People hate to move the big stuff around much because, well, it's heavy. It's smart scouting to go by the yard the night before for a preview of the merchandise. This yard looked to belong to an older couple, and Mister did not look up to moving much heavy furniture. My thought was they'd get the heavy stuff in place and take a good offer early rather than have to move it back. I wanted to be there early enough to offer just below the asking price. You can bargain a bit toward the end of the day on smaller items, but what's the sense in bargaining between a dollar and fifty cents? I have my pride after all.

Anyway, I hung back in the car as the sun came up, watching for any early competitors and to plan my move. There was a dull red Chevy with a torn rag top just across the street. Colerain, (although I did not know his name then), was getting out of this car. He made a beeline for the furniture about 6:20 a.m., so I had to act.

I moseyed over to the three piece set, ran my hand along the fabric and tested the feel of the couch. Cole sat down close to me and gave a bit of a bounce to test the springs. I could tell he was interested … in the furniture. His shoulder brushed me several times as he strayed into my personal space. I'd not been looking for a man for some time and customs may have changed, but his closeness on that couch tagged him as a fast-moving man. But I wanted the furniture. I slid away over to the far edge of the couch to show him my thoughts, then casually felt the fabric on the arm and the headrest. No holes, clean, and no smell or water damage, it was an acceptable piece. Cole felt the same parts of the couch, just in a different order. We were playing a competitive game familiar to any yard sale shoppers. I stood and fake-smiled in Cole's direction and looked over the easy chairs. The older man and woman were still in the house arranging clothes to come out.

Cole trumped me by skipping the chairs and headed to the front door in time to catch the Mister as he came out."

"How much for the furniture? He asked.

"We were thinking one hundred dollars. The pieces are hardly used."

"A fair price, and I love the color. Will you take a check?"

"No, cash only."

"Let me run to the store and get some cash and I'll be right back.

"Technically by Yard Sale Etiquette he was entitled to the pieces as the first bidder. His mistake was that he didn't ask the owner to hold the furniture and just left it open as a possible sale. I smiled as he left and fingered the five twenty dollar bills in my purse. In a few minutes, the deal was done. The Mister was glad to have the cash over a possible later sale. I scouted around a bit to kill some time and felt that pride a person gets over a bargain scooped away from someone else. I went looking for my cousin to help me load the pieces on his trailer. Maybe I was waiting around long enough to watch Cole's face as we loaded the furniture.

His face told me so much about him. He was pleased for me and smiled as he came over to congratulate me on a deal well done. There was not a trace of a fake smile. I knew he must be anxious to get on to another sale for some furniture that would suit his needs, but he stayed and we talked. After an appropriate time, he asked if I wanted to go somewhere for breakfast. I think he suggested Bojangles. I have a weakness for their country ham biscuits, so I said yes.

He's coming for dinner next Saturday. A part of me is looking for those second chances.

Well, now you know, Patsy."

A long-standing disagreement

Growing up in Marsden, Lizzie and Met lived for
dancing but were in different social circles as a black
teen and a white teen. In the South of the 1970s, school
integration was a flashpoint for small Eastern North
Carolina communities with near daily racial flares.
Young adults needed a neutral place to have fun away
from the racial tension. Lizzie, Met, and their groups of
friends found that neutral place at the beachfront shag
clubs in Myrtle Beach, South Carolina. The shag is a
dance native to the Coastal South; for Southern teens of
those turbulent times, dancing was an equalizer. At the
Pavilion in Myrtle Beach there were no color boundaries
if you could dance.

Lizzie sat back on the porch chair and her eyes traced
back over the years and the story unfolded.

"When I was younger, and a lot thinner, I loved to
dance. Dancing was our way of burning energy and
getting noticed by boys. The smoother you could dance,
the more notice you got. My girlfriends and I would
practice for hours dancing with each other or holding a
doorknob as an invisible partner. We might dance some
in Marsden at the St. Moritz, but dance places here were

either all white or all black and the music was not as flashy as it was in Myrtle Beach. Everybody went to Myrtle Beach for serious dancing."

Shag dancing developed in the thirties along the South Carolina coast as black dancers from New York vacationed in quiet Myrtle Beach. In Myrtle Beach in the early 1960s, the shag evolved into a sensual dance. It was called the dirty shag then; pelvic thrusts and all sorts of gyrating against your partner. Dance clubs in Myrtle Beach had to put up fences around their dance floors because locals complained about the blatant sexual moves of the dirty shag. Kids experimenting with the new beat of rock and roll perfected their steps to loud music blaring out of beachfront dance parlors like the Pavilion. Steps got slang names like 'Ozzie's shuffle' or the 'bump, bump, bump' and everyone copied the new steps and adapted them to their own style."

Lizzie smiled as if to share an inside joke about dancing and getting male attention as she continued with her tale.

"My crowd of six boys and girls would drive down to Ocean Drive and stay in some cheap motel far back from the beach. My momma thought we were in separate rooms. We were registered separate, but who paired off and for how long depended on lots of things. The sex part wasn't as important as the dancing; most of the time we were so tired from dancing, and so hot from the humidity, that not much else happened. We came down from Marsden three or four times a year. The dance floor was most crowded in the summer, and summer was just plain hot and sticky. There was no air conditioning in our cheap motel. At the Pavilion, if we were lucky; a breeze blew off the ocean to give some cooling. Everybody and everything was sticky and the bugs were terrible. Black couples and white couples were watching each other, keeping an eye out for new steps. On Friday and Saturday nights music blared out over the beach from ten in the morning till late. After midnight there was no room on the floor, so people danced on the beach or in the streets. Roscoe and I nearly always left when the place closed at two a.m. on Saturday morning, and walked back to the motel. We fell into bed sweaty and exhausted. Drinking was not as important as it is today, mainly because we could not afford the alcohol. For us, every trip was a cheap weekend. The only cost for dancing was change for the jukebox, and there were so many people that you rarely had to use your own money."

Patrice added something about the lines of pancake houses, but Lizzie looked at her as if she were interrupting a carefully-refined story. Lizzie continued:

We loved the Pavilion because it was fast and loose with a high wooden fence around it along the land side so the local church-goers didn't get shocked by our dancing. The beach side was open. Back then it was a magical combination of the place, the crowd, the music, and the energy. I feel that I was at my best back then, and that everything since has been slower. Even today, for me the memory of the beach is the sandy concrete, the blaring jukebox, and the smell and sound of the ocean.

Shag music is simple, but oh so powerful, with words that express deep feelings of love found and love lost, and a regular beat that catches in your brain and stays there long after the song has ended. Anytime I hear beach music, I can't stop my feet moving to the simple one and two, three and four, five, six shag beat. The dance and the music blend perfectly, especially in hot weather. The groups I hear on the radio on Sunday afternoons keep up the tradition pretty well.

Anyway, I knew of Met then and knew he was from Marsden. Back then he made everyone call him E-met for some silly reason, like he was better than the rest of us. Roscoe and I would see him and his girlfriend Peggy on the dance floor. Peggy was tall like him and her eyes had something not truthful about them. To me she'd rolled around in some muddy places in her day and didn't want you to know it. She thought she was pretty hot with skin tight black cutoffs, his cotton shirt knotted around her waist, and her blond hair pulled into a ponytail that bounced as she shagged. I didn't like the attitude of that couple from the beginning and thought their dance style was simple. To be known as a good dancing couple was important.

One Saturday in July we were feeling the spirit of the music and had some extra money for a few beers, and all that tension came to a head. Roscoe, Met, Peggy, all of us thought we were pretty good, and we were, amateur good. ur styles were as different as our skin color. My style was dramatic; with moves some would call *really* dirty shagging. I loved to rub against Roscoe and he'd move me around like I was a puppet. Most times there was not more than an inch between us on the floor. Those were powerful times for a teenage girl because of the loud music and the heat; all with the closeness of your partner and a sense of abandon. The music and the beat made you want to be pressed together and to grind against each other, as the beat took over your brain. Met's style was less passionate than mine and more like shagging today, with frequent leg pops with twirls and belly rolls woven into the intricate extra steps that he worked into the simple count. On any weekend in Myrtle Beach you could watch endless variations of the two styles.

I can still remember that steamy July night like it was yesterday. Met must have been feeling feisty, because he danced right up next to us as he and Peggy tried to mirror our moves. Then they moved away and he said something to her and both smiled at each other, like they were talking about us. That smirk hit me wrong, and at that time in my life, I took it personal like they were mocking our dancing. After a few minutes, the moment passed and they went back to their smooth moves and smiled in our direction. Then Met took to staring at us as his smile got wider, almost like he was challenging us, claiming he was better than we were. To tell it now sounds silly, but back then it was serious to challenge another couple like that on their dancing. Roscoe did not even notice all the drama I was feeling. He was moving to his own beat with a few beers in him and waving to his friends as we danced, but I was watching those two and picked up Met's intentions right away. The song finished and Met and Peggy left the floor. He made a special point of grinning at me as they passed and gave a little cocky tilt of his head as if to say, now that's how it's done lady. Well, I grabbed Roscoe, and we headed out to the floor for the next song. Even though the shag is a man's dance, and the woman's role is to follow his lead, I put some moves on Roscoe that made me proud. The night was right, the song was perfect, and I had the moves. I knew Met was watching and I cut my eyes at him to give back a taste of that grin he'd given me.

We were good on that dance, emotions stoked by the night and the heat. Maybe I danced better because I was on a mission to prove to that white boy that the shag was a black dance first and foremost and there won't gonna be no white boy upping me on it. After all the work I'd put him through, poor Roscoe needed a rest. He'd risen to the challenge and pressed and moved over near every part of my body, and we were covered in sweat. If any of my family would have seen me, they'd have disowned me for doing the dirty shag and looking trashy, but I had something to prove.

Met walked over to us and started it all up again by showing that grin that just set me on edge, because I knew it was fake. He started with,

'Nice dancing. You two are a good looking couple.'

Roscoe looked a little dazed, because although whites and blacks spoke some, it was never in that friendly a way.

'Thank you' was all he could muster. He was pretty subdued for Roscoe, but then he'd missed all those eye cuts and snarky grinning that had set me on edge and was a little off because I'd worked him so hard. I had a lot more I wanted to say, and maybe it was the beer, or maybe it was just that time for me, but I almost let fly with something about him being a fool for thinking he was a better dancer. I held my piece and regret it to this day, because that was the perfect time to launch all those feelings.

'You dance about as good as we do,' Met needling me again. 'It's good to see good dancers on the floor'. I thought he was going to launch into a discussion of our style or ask if he could use one of the steps we'd developed. If it would have ended there, that would have been fine. Roscoe might even have taken Peggy out to the floor and showed her one of our ordinary steps, and Met might have done the same with me and shocked the crowd at the Pavilion with two mixed couples. But that

Met has an evil side, and he didn't act like a normal person."

Met leaned over to Roscoe and said, in a voice entirely too loud for the occasion. "Would you care to dance for a bet? Just the two couples and we can make it for twenty dollars to the winner, or if you only have ten dollars … or just for any amount you want."

Roscoe just stared at this brazen white boy. Although there might be some friendly competition between white couples or black couples, he had never heard of such an obvious dancing challenge. One thing I can say about Roscoe is that he loves a challenge. Deep down, he knew we were better dancers and he wanted to show this boy that it was true and wanted every person in the crowd in the Pavilion on that Saturday night to know it too.

Roscoe stood up close to him and said, 'We'll take your money. How about if we flip a coin and the winner can pick the song? I'll set it up on the jukebox. When it comes on, we'll start.' It didn't take any time for the club to hear about the bet, and people came over to talk and show support. We were pretty surprised to even have some white couples come over and wish us luck. Fat Harold, the owner, stopped people putting money in the jukebox and everything got real quiet all of a sudden. In the silence, everyone gathered around the floor and Harold introduced the four of us. He explained the simple rules: we both were on the floor at the same time to the same song with an applause vote at the end. Loudest applause won bragging rights.

Roscoe won the toss and picked one of our favorite songs, fast and loose enough to show off our moves, but not so fast that the audience would miss the fancy footwork. Roscoe not only was a good dancer, but he knew how to play the audience. He started slow with some ordinary twirls and spins, then moved into his signature move, a foot roll from heel to toe, and then wowed them with a boogie walk with his knees flapping out to the sides as fast as the music played. I kept the beat and let him lead. We knew that to win we'd have to get into more dirty shag, because Met wouldn't, so I moved into him as he ground his pelvis on mine and ran his hands all over me while making eye contact with every woman in the crowd. It felt great and we were on, almost professional. I couldn't see Met and Peggy's moves, but from the audience hoots and whistles coming from our side, it seemed they liked our style best. The only fancy things I saw from them were a few fast pivots and some belly rolls. As Met saw us getting dirty, his belly rolls became more intense and even stiff Peggy got into it and pulled her ponytail out and her hair fly out to the sides as he pivoted her.

The song ended and Roscoe took his dishrag out of his back pocket and wiped beads of sweat off his forehead. As a good Southern girl, I'd never sweat, but my skin glistened with a glow after that dance. Neither Met nor Peggy seemed to have much of a sweat on. Peggy stood

beside him and smiled kind of dumb-like and looked
around the audience, hoping for their applause. She may
have been a fair dancer, but she was not a brain, and
certainly not a beauty.

Judging time. The DJ put us at either end of the floor.
He went to Met and Peggy first, and the audience
applauded wildly with hoots and whistles from every
part of the club. The he came to us, and the audience
applauded even louder, a surprise since there were a lot
more whites than blacks in the room. This is where it got
complicated. I was pretty sure they had clapped for us
louder by far, but Met was sure that his audience
response was louder. He raised his arms as the winner,
and twirled Peggy to signify that they'd won. Roscoe
and I were so shocked that we just stood still and looked
at Fat Harold for his judgment. But the crowd mobbing
the floor along with the noise and Met whirling Peggy
drowned out anything Harold may have said.

Well, that's the story, and I'm still convinced that he
stole the contest. That poor soul Roscoe never recovered
from the embarrassment of being beaten by a white boy,
and stopped shagging altogether. I continued dancing
and still enjoy a dance today, but if that skunk Met is in
the room, I won't go on the dance floor."

Reverend Millie

Scruffie was a loyal cat. He'd stayed with me through three husbands, and now part way through the fourth. A few weeks back, he was looking a bit mopey and wasn't eating well. He'd always been a picky eater, as cats can be. Because of his seniority, he ate only gourmet cat food, and preferred his food warmed in the microwave. Cats can have a moodiness about them even in the best of times, but I was worried about him not eating.

I'd been out running errands and when I came in the side door, there lay Scruffie stretched out on the kitchen floor, nearly on his back. He did not look good at all; in fact, he looked dead. I called my husband, Glenn, for confirmation. Through our married life, he's been the official judge of dead animals in the household. Glenn smoothed the cold fur, tried to move his stiff legs as well as they would move, felt his chest, and gave his verdict.

"Well Millie, I'm afraid he's gone. I know that's hard for you to accept, but he's seemed a little puny over the past few weeks. I didn't want to worry you. Looks like he had something wrong, something seriously wrong." It was the middle of January during one of those cold spells that Marsden gets. The ground was frozen and so the burial had to be delayed.

Glenn had not liked Scruffie from the day we started courting, so I wasn't surprised that no more was said about planning a burial service. But I had to do something with the corpse until the ground thawed. I found a big plastic bag with a zipper closure, slid Scruffie into the bag and put him way in the back of the outdoor freezer. Glenn didn't need to know. The only things in there were deer meat, a few bear steaks Glenn had gotten from one of his hunting buddies, and soft shell crabs we'd caught off the pier last fall.

It was a busy winter, and I forgot about Scruffie until about April when we had a craving for crabs. At first it was hard to recognize what was in that big bag in the back with frost around the edges, but I recognized the bag and the zipper. Glenn is good about writing labels with dates on the bags so we know how long the deer or bear meat has been frozen, so this wasn't one of Glenn's bags. It was a very frosty Scruffie. I pulled him out of the freezer and then out of the bag. Luckily, we have a counter off the kitchen, and I could use that as a preparation site. The remains were cold and stiff with his legs angled out and fur matted to his body. He did have a kind of smile on his face though, a reminder that passing over the mystical plane into death may not be all that bad an experience if you can go with it. I couldn't bring myself to bury him frozen, so he needed to come back to room temperature for his cleanup. My sense of decency and loyalty would not let me bury him looking so, well, scruffy. By evening, the thawed Scruffie was soggy, and a smell rose up that gave an urgency to the burial service. Glenn had come to investigate the smell. To his credit, he nodded and held his usual smart comments, then shook his head and went inside.

My challenge was to make Scruffie presentable. I got a hair dryer and started to work on his fur, combing and straightening it to look like it had looked in life. Cleaning dead bodies requires some experience, and I did not have much, but I worked along as if I were styling a customer in the shop. I find that work goes easier if you chat a little with the customer, but Scruffie didn't have anything to say. Liberal use of hair spray kept his fur in place and helped with the smell. I asked Glenn to hold him up so I could dry and style the under part, but he refused, so I could only work on his upside. His upside was the only part that was going to show anyway. After two cans of hairspray and considerable styling, he looked presentable enough to be buried. I lined a big UPS box with a pretty flowered bath towel and arranged Scruffie in the box. If I bent his head or his legs, I was worried they'd snap, so I settled on positioning his legs angled out as if he were in mid-run. In that position, he was longer and wider than I'd estimated and seemed to be all legs. I located a larger box. I didn't like the postal labels and stamps on the front, which seemed disrespectful, but it was all I had to work with. When he was arranged on the bath towel, good side up, I closed the lid, taped it shut for his privacy, and carried the coffin to the yard.

Glenn had been wandering around the house for days with not much to do, and I put him on a grave-digging detail. The sunny spot behind the house was perfect, and as he dug, he grumbled about the tree roots and stopped digging when he hit water. Marsden has a low water table, so a few feet down was as far as we were likely to get. We looked over the hole and saw that the box was larger by about six inches on each side, so Glenn had to do more digging while Scruffie and I waited for the ceremony. The bottom of the hole had about an inch of standing water, so I put a roasting grill in to keep Scruffie's coffin out of the water then knelt and lowered him into the grave. I liked the spot Glenn picked because it got morning sun most of the year, and Scruffie had some of his better days lying in the sun. I thought he would enjoy that spot for eternity.

I'd never preached at a cat funeral before, but I managed some kind words about what a good cat he'd been and how I hoped he was in a better place. I tried to remember specifics about his life, but he had died long enough ago that none came to mind. I believe in reincarnation, so I'm sure Scruffie will be recycling back to the world in some other form, hopefully more advanced than his cat self. Kneeling beside the grave, I missed any mystical moments of his soul passing out of his body. After all, he'd been dead for four months and any passing of his soul had happened long before. Glenn was supportive, but quiet. We held hands and he offered a few words about Scruffie resting in peace in the sunshine and about the circle of life. To his credit, he did not put on one of those smirks he can get.

Burial is a closure, and I needed the ceremony to close my link with Scruffie. If the situation had been reversed, he would have treated me as kindly. The sun broke through the clouds as I walked back to the house and Glenn piled on the dirt. There was no need to shed tears. I'd done right by Scruffie.

Ro-Ro and Pipi have a tiff

In the heady early days of our relationship, we joked about nicknames and came up with the wildest (for us) we could think of, Ro-Ro and Pipi. We took it far enough one year to dress in these alter egos for a Halloween party. I (Ro-Ro) went as a biker bad boy and Pipi was a preppy California girl drawn to the bad boy. That night we won, as much for the names as for the costumes.

The South is a cornucopia of nicknames that usually sound better tagged to young girls. When a young girl acquires a nickname, it travels with her throughout her life. I met a charming mature woman named Sunny-Lou downtown on my morning walk. My favorite format is the two first names like Leigh-Leigh, Mary Sue, Betty Ann and the like. Men's names don't sound nearly as charming, but the names often describe the man. You'll meet Southern men named Cooter, Dog, Pie, or the ever-popular Bubba, and of course Met. It's hard for anyone to know how the nicknames came about, but Dog admitted his came from his love for Will's Hot Dogs and a teenage contest where he ate a dozen fully dressed Will's Dogs in ten minutes. An alternative to the descriptive name for men is shortening the name to initials, such as AJ, JP, or TOB. My favorite Southern male name is T-Ray, a nice blend of both worlds. I think if we ever get a dog, T-Ray would be its name, unless Pipi wins and calls him Bob.

But I digress. It would not be a fair representation in these stories about our lives in the South to ignore a common phenomenon between men and women—a tiff. The best definition of a tiff is an accelerated disagreement, more severe and longer than an argument yet less intense than a knock-down, drag out fight. In our relationship, a tiff happens when there is too much closeness. People are not meant to live together in close quarters for hundreds of hours, it causes them to chafe. I suspect that Northerners in isolated parts of Alaska or Minnesota living in a one room home during the long hours of winter darkness have a lot of tiffs, even if it's yelling at their companion dog or cat.

For us, a tiff is needed about every three to four months. The action part is short-lived because of our personalities which are more the long fuse and quick blow types. Overall, we come out of it feeling much better. There is something about re-establishing a neutral baseline that makes a tiff a therapeutic event. Tiffs can come up like a summer storm on the river, unexpected and intense, or can slowly build after some insignificant slight earlier in the day with a spark igniting the air in a fiery climax. Sharp words spoken in heat may cause wounds; but in this particular tiff the words were muffled by the emotional storm. I suspect everyone reading knows a tiff in their own relationship.

This is written several days after the tiff. I've carefully edited any emotion out so there is no polarization. Let me set the scene. Patrice and I had been gone for a week, riding home from a recent trip to the western part of the state. The economy being as it is, driving seemed like the most practical way to get away and see the beautiful western part of North Carolina. Even with a frugal trip, fuel was a hundred dollars each way! We were laughing about our nicknames and what our Southern friends might think of them; pleasant conversation passing easily on a road trip. Things quickly turned terribly wrong. Patrice decided to stop at a large farmer's market to shop for produce. That stop led to the tiff...

The details are so silly when put to paper, but the details are seldom what the tiff is about. It started, as such things often do, by an unintentional miscommunication. Something like: "she said and I thought she said." In this case, person A was to pick up person B at a location and time thought by A to have been agreed upon. Person A arrived thirty minutes later than B expected. B was furious, foaming, sputtering, and calling up all manner of past baggage. Everything from "don't you have a watch?" to "can't you tell time" and that favorite old chestnut "you always do this to me." Person A is taken aback by the fury because the time had been agreed upon and A is on time. Further, A went out of their way to pick up several tasty treats for B as a surprise for the long drive home. Those are the basics, but there is an endless variety of tone and pitch and body language. The events are, in retrospect, a simple misunderstanding. Under normal circumstances such misunderstandings would be overlooked, but today those events advanced into a tiff.

The next phase of the tiff usually depends on the personal comfort level riding in the car. In Eastern Carolina, hunger, fatigue, heat, and humidity are favorites for discomfort. In other climates you can substitute snow, rain, fog, mosquitoes, or any other significant inconvenience and the effect would be the same.

You've seen those creative children's books that ask the reader to substitute a word or phrase in the sentence to change the story line. Returning to our tiff, readers can do a similar substitution of phrases or reactions thinking about their last tiff. What happens in this phase is what makes each tiff so individual.

- A refuses to speak to B until there is an apology. Time drags on.

- Tempers of A and B flare, the flames burn brightly until both come back to baseline after less than thirty minutes.

- B continues venting out of frustration for "all the past times you've done this" for another hour or so while A tunes it all out and focuses on driving.

- B takes the treat, smiles sweetly with genuine gratitude, and all is back to normal in a few minutes.

And then there is the popular reaction:

- A takes it personally, brings up all of B's past times of doing the "exact same thing," and pouts until the next morning when things return to normal with a smile and a hug initiated by either A or B.

My momma always used to preach to my younger brother and me that two people should never go to sleep angry. In her mind, this rule applied to couples even more so. To her, disagreements had to be settled before sleep, because any pent-up negativity held over till morning was not healthy.

Gosh it's hard to follow her advice at times, but we managed yet again. All is well with Ro-Ro and Pipi for another night.

Sprouts

The fork and I waltzed the three remaining Brussels sprouts around the melamine plate like synchronized ice skaters, tracing the floral pattern ever slower. The repeated scraping had quickly become irritating to all of us around an otherwise silent dinner table.

In the 1950s, our family tradition was to gather at the dinner table for conversation and fellowship. On this Wednesday evening, we five sat at the table, sharing the events of the day, with mother leading and my younger brother and sister squirming in their seats. Spring had come to South Boston and they wanted to be outside. At nine, I had come into an age of rebellion and found the nightly family dinner a terrible bore, but the house rule was that if you didn't come to dinner at the table, nothing else was offered. "You'll eat with your family, or you won't eat at all," my mother would say, peppered liberally with phrases such as, "I'll serve it, you'll eat it, and you'll like it."

During this phase of my childhood, mother's cooking incorporated a combination of canned corn, canned peas, or canned carrots as a dinner side dish with occasional seasonal fresh vegetables. Frozen vegetables were a convenience still in the future, as was the microwave. Over the past year, she came to believe that our family did not eat a balanced diet of fresh vegetables. When the local grocery ran a sale on Brussels sprouts, she bought a pound to compliment her pot roast for dinner. Brussels sprouts were considered an avant-garde vegetable, and mother wanted us to try them. I'm sure she had not cooked sprouts. Her technique was that nothing would be undercooked. She boiled the mini cabbages until they were a mushy greenish-gray and considered them cooked just perfectly. At her table, foods were eaten as served, with any added salt or pepper a backhanded slight to the cook. She proudly placed four green-gray balls on each of our plates as she told us about sprouts and emphasized their nutritional value. She pointed out that the four small sprouts would provide an enormous amount of vitamins for our growing bodies.

Dinner continued with pot roast and rolls added to the sprouts. Everyone cleaned their plates and was anxious to leave, but my dance continued with the remaining three mushy sprouts on my plate. With each twist of the fork, I could feel the thick, mushy, bland sensation in the back of my throat from the first sprout; I couldn't swallow another without an embarrassing event. Tension settled around the table like evening fog on the river. Dinner was not finished until everyone had cleaned their plate and our father dismissed us. Mother's glare bored into my forehead from across the table and my father leaned back in his chair, waiting with increasing discomfort. My brother jabbed my sister under the table, and they snickered behind their hands while enjoying the standoff. Both had finished their allotted four sprouts and watched my discomfort, calculating how my mother would adjudicate the standoff. I hoped my father would tire of the drama and dismiss us, but the glances between him and my mother implied there was a principle to be learned. Even though I was the oldest, and nearly grown at nine, we were still a family; the family had rules, and the rule of eating your vegetables would be enforced.

The plate looked enormous, bare with only the three wilted balls. I nixed the obvious solution of accidentally tipping the plate onto the floor; my mother would see right through that ploy, dust off the fallen sprouts, and place them back in front of me. The standoff continued. For the fifth time, my mother prodded, "Just cut one in half, put it on your fork, and eat it. It's not poison, you know. I would never have you eat something that was bad for you. The *Reader's Digest* says that Brussels sprouts are good for you; they have a lot of iron, and you need that extra iron to help you grow."

I looked to my father for mercy. We had a growing male bond since he started working as a little league announcer for my games, but there was no mercy. "Do what your mother says and finish the three on your plate, then you can go," he spoke kindly, but firmly.

My brother jabbed my sister again under the table and covered his mouth as he laughed and whispered something, probably something about what a wimp I was. I would get him for that later. As the youngest and the only girl, my sister did not laugh, and I could feel her sympathy across the table. Minutes passed and my arm ached from pushing the fork around the plate. Something had to be done, and I was out of ideas. Maybe if I gagged on the half, I could get out of eating the rest.

Out of the blue, salvation came. My brother reached across my plate, speared two of the balls on his fork, and ate them. My sister kneeled on her chair and reached across the table, an etiquette violation in my mother's book, speared the remaining sprout, and ate it just as quickly. My father looked at my mother for a decision on this unexpected turn of events. She nodded almost imperceptibly.

"We're dismissed, thank your mother for preparing this meal." The classical ending from my father. Chairs were pushed back, and my brother and sister jostled each other to get outside. I looked to my mother for guidance. She smiled a smile of love, a smile of understanding. Behind that smile I read that our family had tried Brussels sprouts, once. Something in her smile worried me about what avant-garde vegetable she might try next.

Julia and the ducks

Mother's death devastated Julia, and the end of
caregiving magnified her loss. She knew little about
grieving, especially grieving from the deep loss of such
an important part of herself. In Marsden she had few
close friends and stumbled through as best she could,
waking up each morning to the loss, living the day, and
remembering. She cared for Blanche after the stroke
because she was the only daughter and daughters are
ready to come in times of need. Caregiving is the legacy
of daughters. Sons move away and raise families, while
daughters remain linked to their mothers throughout life.

Blanche had been spunky until her first stroke. Although
the only residual damage was a minor limp, the illness
produced frailty, and this newly frail person needed
care. Shortly after Julia moved in, Blanche's personality
regressed as her frustration and depression grew. "An
illness can sap a strong person's will to live, and your
mother may never recover either her strength or her
personality," advised the Hospice nurses, and Julia saw
the steady decline with each passing day. They had been
close when her mother was healthy, each woman
gradually finding the right balance between a mother

and daughter trying to live independent lives. Blanche and Julia visited often, usually for lunch, and supported each other with quiet talks in good times and bad. People at the funeral commented on the strength of their relationship; how it must have benefited both women without constraining either. Julia nodded politely at their expected comments that Blanche was in a better place.

She started to feed the ducks about a month after she buried her mother, maybe as her own way of grieving. Ducks swim in the protected creek outside downtown Marsden and this situation is a near-perfect match: tame ducks fed by grandparents and young children. Julia had always seen ducks in the creek but had not felt a need to feed them until a sunny morning in June. She had been thinking about Blanche's last days. During her morning walks, Julia stopped to watch the ducks, and the next morning brought scraps of bread. A flock of mallards was swimming in the middle of the creek and changed course to intersect her on shore. The group waddled up the bank for their familiar feeding routine. Julia noticed distinctive personalities, aggressive ones at the front and the more cautious toward the back. She watched them jostle for their share, but noticed that one female waited apart from the group. This white duck with a black swatch across its chest waddled around the perimeter of the group, not interested in the bread, and seemed to watch Julia. There was something vaguely familiar about this duck.

If she let her imagination run, Julia could see a familiar close-cropped haircut, a distinctive slouching walk with a slight limp in the right leg, and a gimlet stare. She stopped tearing bread as the outlandish idea came into her mind that this duck could be her mother reincarnated. She tried to push the idea away, but it stayed as an odd image of her momma and the duck, faces and bodies superimposed. *Ridiculous*, she thought. *It's natural to be thinking about her; what with the care she needed after the second stroke, days in a coma, and finally, that painful decision to stop life support.* Julia was sitting beside Blanche when she passed quietly in the hour before dawn, their hands linked until one went limp and fell away onto the bed.

Her thoughts came back to the ducks. *To be sure, I must be imagining it. What kind of daughter sees her dead mother reincarnated as a mallard?* Still, the familiarity was unsettling. As if to reinforce a possible kinship, the duck approached Julia and stopped several feet in front of her. Julia laughed as she talked to the duck.

"You remind me of my momma. Bet that's the first time you've heard that line. Well, I don't usually talk to ducks, but I'm going to call you Clementine, because that was my momma's name." She laughed at how Momma hated her given name. In her mind, the name Clementine evoked trite images of the old west; ranchers' daughters in gingham dresses, cattle, and campfires. Her mother preferred to be called Blanche, a racy name she chose during her young adulthood because the sound of it rolled off the tongue. The name Blanche better matched her personality—a bit on the edge, independent, and outgoing.

Julia was busy through the week and did not get back to the creek until Monday morning. The flock approached from the water as she pulled into the parking area. Clementine remained on the edge of the group, wary and standoffish. She fed the ducks nearly a half loaf of bread and looked around for Clementine, but the duck remained at the back of the group, looking at Julia. *Just like Momma, an attitude early in the morning.*

Julia thought maybe she should be more understanding. *If this duck was indeed Momma sent back to Earth for some reason, she must have had quite a trip. The horrific strain of dying, passing over the river Styx in that leaky boat with that creepy boatman, standing before God in judgment, and then after all that, waking to find her soul in a duck's body. That was a story Momma would love to tell her friends at Bunko night.*

Julia puzzled over the possibilities; with all the space in the world and in the beyond, why would God place her momma beside this creek in Marsden. *Was there some plan in having us cross paths?* Finally, she sat down on the creek bank, dropped the remaining bread, and tried to sort it out. Julia was not good at fitting together such big thoughts, but the more she considered it, the more the situation seemed strangely logical, perhaps even destined. God and Her plan for the world came to mind.

Throughout her life, she had not had much personal interaction with God, but believed in the basics. *There was a God and She cared about people. This scene was exactly how She might choose a sign. Wasn't the bible full of stories of God striking people off horses and appearing as burning bushes and on fiery chariots? There were no burning bushes around Marsden, but something like this might be my personal sign from God. I suppose it might happen that way, but it was beyond strange. What can I possibly learn from a duck?*

She looked to Clementine for an answer. The duck stood apart from the flock, preening her feathers. *Well, that makes sense, how would she know I was thinking about her? She can't read my mind, now can she?* She tried another approach to communicating and called out to all the ducks in the flock, "Clementine, Clementine" to see if the duck might recognize the name. Luckily there was no one around at the time to hear her talking to the flock of ducks. *Surely if the duck was her mother reincarnated, she would make some sign that she understood, even maybe an angry sign that she hated that name.* As if reacting to the name, Clementine looked in her direction, tilted her head to the side and extended her beak toward Julia, a possible sign she was responding to the name. Julia tried turning around, facing away from the ducks, and softly spoke the name Blanche, just once, and with as much love as she had spoken it to her mother on her deathbed. She turned quickly and to her the duck seemed happier with a kind of duck smile on her upturned beak. The other ducks continued their morning routine and wandered back to the water. This name test clinched it for Julia. This duck was her momma sure and definitely did not like the name Clementine.

Julia pushed on to see if duck and daughter could communicate. She broke off a piece of bread and held it in her open palm and Blanche slowly approached. Julia held the bread in her palm and the duck extended her beak and snapped at the bread. It took some trial and error to get the technique refined so that Blanche could take the bread without nipping Julia's palm. The duck had an unsettling way of looking into Julia's eyes, trying for some form of communication. Eventually, Blanche waddled away, her right leg dragging just a bit. This was typical of her mother in life; when she finished a conversation, she just left. Julia detected a sarcastic kind of a squawk as Blanche turned at the water's edge and swam off, an indication that the interaction had ended. Julia tried to fit these confusing experiences into something that made sense.

The next morning, common sense dominated. *It just is not likely that Momma's a duck, and even more unlikely that she would appear here in Marsden where I would find her. None of this makes any sense. Isn't my mind just trying to grieve and I am seeing her all around me as a subconscious reminder?* Still, the duck did remind her of her momma. *All right. I'll go back and see if she is still there, but I cannot imagine she would be.* This

time she took a fresh loaf of bread. Just in case this duck
was her momma, Julia would not want to be
inconsiderate by bringing stale bread. There was no one
at the creek bank this early, but the ducks were waiting
for someone to feed them. She spotted Blanche behind
the group and imagined a look from her, grateful Julia
had come back. She tore the bread and tossed it to the
ducks as Blanche watched from the edge of the group.
The ducks ate their fill and moved away, leaving the
remaining bread uneaten. Blanche waddled up in front
of Julia and made a kind of grunting sound as if
prodding Julia to say something. Julia felt silly talking to
a duck, but said the first thing that popped into her mind.

"Good morning, Momma."

"Quack."

"Well, you have to admit this is pretty silly, talking to a
duck, even if you might be my momma."

"Quack."

"I'm not doubting that it's you talking to me as a duck,
but I'm going to need some convincing that you're my
mother before I continue this conversation. All you can
do is quack anyway, so how can we communicate?"

"Quack."

"Here's a test to see if you're really are my momma.
People go to a séance to communicate with the dead and
to ask them questions. Let's see if you can answer this

question. I lost a locket about a year ago; it was my favorite piece of jewelry. You remember that it was the heart-shaped one with our picture in it, standing outside church on a sunny morning. We were so happy together that morning. One day the locket was gone. We both looked for it, but never found it. I was sad, and you were angry over my carelessness."

"Quack."

"Tell me where to find that locket? You probably have some special powers, being dead and all, that let you know things living people don't know."

There was no response from the duck, but a vivid image formed somewhere in Julia's mind. The image took shape as a moving picture, in sharp focus and vivid color. She saw herself standing in her bedroom, and the image shifted to the dresser against the wall. Magically, the dresser moved away from the wall, and Julia saw the glint of the locket hanging from its chain behind the dresser, dangling out of sight on a small nail.

Now this is creepy, thought Julia. *Did you send that image into my mind; can you communicate through some kind of mental power? If so, that is so cool.* She drove home and believed she would find the locket exactly where she had seen it in her vision. She burst through the front door, ran across the hall to the bedroom, and stopped in front of the dresser. She inched it away from the wall enough to look behind it. The locket was there, dangling from a nail, as it had been in the vision. She reached down and took it, pressing it close to her heart, then looked to the heavens and mouthed a silent thank you to God, or Blanche, for recovering the precious memento. All through the day her mind kept cycling back to the vivid images that appeared in her mind just after she asked the question about the locket.

In protest, her practical side took over. *If Blanche knew where the locket had been lost, what else might she know? Did she have a way of stealing into my memories? Did she know about the affair I had with Jason Briley. Did she know about the time I stayed out late drinking and tried a puff of grass when I was home from college? Did she know about a hundred other things I've kept secret from her?* Even if she knew about any of those things, what difference would it possibly make? She was a duck and couldn't do anything now. Julia laughed to herself because she knew her mother would be furious about Jason, because she never liked him. *Now I don't like him either, but back then it seemed to be the right thing to do.* Her practical side took a new track. *Maybe she's trying to help me, maybe to get me to the city where I can get a good job designing clothing. She always encouraged me to use that talent, but I had to stay close to her. There are no jobs in clothing design in small-town Marsden. Maybe finding the locket was a coincidence. Perhaps I knew where it was all the time and just now remembered it. I need to give her a challenging test, one that will convince me that she has exceptional mental powers. If she answers correctly, then maybe those powers can help me.*

The rest of the day she played with possible questions, questions that would require specific knowledge that her momma could not have known in life, but could tap into from the beyond. She lay awake puzzling over the perfect question, and the next morning she still had not settled on one. There were so many possibilities that might help her, from work to love to money. *One answer I really want to know is whom I will marry and how I will meet him.* After a sleepless night, she was in such a tizzy that she skipped putting on her makeup and drove back to the creek faster than she intended. She knew her momma had never left the house without makeup and would disapprove of her coming out without it, but she was willing to face the anger of a duck. When she pulled into the parking lot, everything was as she had left it yesterday, bright summer sun and the flock of ducks waiting for bread.

She did not care much about the other ducks waddling up for bread, and spotted Blanche off to the side. She went through her bread, and the flock was full after a half loaf and moved away. Blanche came into the space where the flock had been and looked at Julia. *If she had the knowledge of where the locket was, surely she can read minds and knows that I have been thinking all night.* Blanche opened the conversation.

"Quack."

Did that mean to go ahead and ask any question, or was it Momma's way of starting a conversation? She always had been a direct one, not wanting to spend any time in pleasantries.

"Quack."

No suitable question had come to Julia's mind after her night of thinking. Then a shadowy image flitted across her mind and formed into an idea. "Okay, Momma, what are the winning lottery numbers? I just saw on TV that the Mega Millions prize is a whopper. I'll go right now and get the ticket with those numbers. If you're right, I'll take you away from here and we'll move to Charlotte."

"Quack."

Almost a soon as she'd spoken the words, Julia saw an image of the Mega Millions board; numbers lit in neon as 45-34-46-25-49-34, as clear as if she'd seen it on television. She jumped at the vivid image, and then got flustered because she didn't have a pen or paper. She ran back to the car, got a pen, and copied the numbers exactly as she had seen them. When she finished writing, the image vanished.

"Thank you, Momma. I have to go get that ticket. Believe me, this is gonna help both of us." She drove to the nearest Hess station and picked the Mega Millions numbers she had written. It was Monday and the next drawing was on Wednesday night. The tally board at the register said this jackpot was sixty-two million dollars.

The days dragged by till the drawing on Wednesday. Julia sat rigid in front of her television at 11:59 p.m. waiting for the announcement of the winning numbers. As the numbers flashed on the screen, one set at a time, she could not believe it. None of the numbers matched. She tried different combinations, but saw none of her numbers in the winning set. Angry and frustrated, she sat immobile. Then she had an epiphany. *To be sure, Momma must be laughing at me for my greed and vanity. How many lectures has she given on avoiding the seven deadly sins? Greed and vanity were right on top of her list of sins to avoid. Of course Momma knew the winning numbers, and just to teach me a lesson, it would be just like her to give me the wrong numbers.* Julia had seldom shown any anger towards her mother, but she felt like driving right back to the creek in the middle of the night and talking with Blanche. Maybe the duck would be there and maybe she would not, but Julia needed to vent her frustration. Out of spite, she did not go to the creek for the next week. *If she thinks tricking me is so funny, then she can just laugh it up all by herself for all I care.*

Days passed and she stewed more and more about the numbers. Well, the ticket was only five dollars, she thought. On Sunday morning, on the way back from church, she drove to the Hess station to get gas. As she was paying at the register, she saw the Mega Millions numbers from the Saturday night drawing and recognized them as the ones she had chosen the previous week. *Well, I'll be damned, Momma had been right after all. I'd just been in such a rush to get that money that I bought the ticket a week too soon.* Not winning sixty-two million is no small disappointment, but Julia was able to find some irony. *I was greedy to get the money, and really, Momma had not told me which week the numbers would match.* It was a lesson like her mother would have taught.

The next morning Julia went back, penitent, with her loaf of bread. There was an elderly man on the far bank fishing for nothing in particular. He was far enough back that he would not hear her talking to Blanche. Julia started talking in a tone she hoped was humble, but slightly peeved, "Well, you were right and you know it, so go ahead and gloat. You know me so well that I get wrapped up in things and rush off to do something before I've had time to think. Now just how was I to know what week you were imaging? It's not like there was a date on the numbers in the image."

"Quack."

"Yes, quack yourself. You were right as usual and I was wrong—again. Moreover, if you know about Jason, I do not need any comments about that either. I was old enough to choose and old enough to know better."

"Quack."

"Well, I don't think we'll try the Mega Millions thing again. That was more stress than I need, and even if I had won the money, that much money can change a person. I like who I am, so I'm not going to ask you to show me how to get lots of money. Besides, I could not take you to Charlotte anyway. You're a duck after all. What would the neighbors think? Let's try another approach to this communication thing. Tell me something about you that I don't know?"

"Quack."

As quickly as before, an image appeared. Her mother's bedroom came into focus, and then the view zoomed to the dresser next to the bed. Julia had not cleaned out her mom's stuff and so things were pretty much as they had been when she was alive. In her vision, the dresser drawer opened and she saw a jumbled stack of pill bottles in the drawer. As if seen through a magnifying lens, one bottle jumped into sharp focus.

"Now that's a puzzle. I guess you want me to go to the dresser, rummage through those bottles, and pick out the one you have shown me. Why does that matter? All right, I asked for a secret and this is your way of telling me one."

She drove to the house; as she opened the door, she felt the damp smell of a closed house. She had never liked Blanche's decorating style, and now the heavy furnishings seemed to exude a musty feel. Pushing on as instructed, Julia went to the bedroom and opened the dresser drawer. Sorting through the ten or so bottles did not take long and she found the bottle she had seen in sharp focus. As she looked at the empty bottle and then at the label, she wondered what was so secret. The bottle was neatly labeled: Clementine Beasly, the dispensing pharmacist, and the medication, Coumadin. Coumadin, a blood thinner had been the crucial medication her mom had been taking to prevent a future stroke. The prescription was filled six weeks before her mom died, the number of tablets dispensed was thirty and there were three refills.

Nothing unusual. Then the beginning of an understanding came. If Momma had been taking the medication as directed, she would have run out of pills two weeks before she had the stroke. There were no other bottles of Coumadin in the drawer. Julia felt a shiver as the puzzle pieces clicked into place. Blanche died of a recurrent stroke, a stroke that happened because she had not refilled her medication. A fateful choice that she had kept to herself.

Images of understanding and profound sorrow flooded Julia's mind as she sank to the bed. Blanche had always been a competent woman, so not refilling medication was a careful choice and not forgetfulness. Julia recalled Blanche's frustration with the limp after the first stroke, the long period of rehabilitation, and taking a medication that gave her bruises if she bumped into anything.

Julia drove back to the creek, forming a conversation in her mind, to say so much and hopefully to hear so much. The ducks were waiting, but Blanche was gone. She never saw that duck again.

The creek

Geography separates Marsden into the part that floods and the part that doesn't. Most of the city is at sea level, and the town ditch, a drainage canal that meanders through downtown, separates high ground from low ground. Days of hurricane winds blowing from the northeast forces water up the river, quickly flooding the ditch and surrounding properties on the low side of town. Helpless property owners watch the water rise during a storm, over the foundation and then pouring into the lower floors of their homes, destroying their property. When the storm passes, the water runs out, leaving both the land and the homes a muddy mess. To help alleviate flooding, engineering experts installed a pump system at the end of the town ditch. During a storm, pumps remove rainwater runoff from low-lying areas and deposit it in the short segment of the creek between the river and the Main Street Bridge known as Jackson's Creek. The name is not listed on any city documents, but comes from local history. This is one version of the naming of the creek.

Jackson Anderson Henry Cooper was a character. Around Marsden, that made for interesting living. He was a dabbler all his life, holding down interesting jobs and then telling robust, often ribald stories about his adventures. In Marsden, Coop was always addressed by his last name, perhaps to distinguish him from his brother, John. The brothers were identical twins, but with different personalities.

John and Coop grew up in the country around Eastern North Carolina. The family farm became more of a losing business with wet weather for a few years followed by dry weather for a few more. When the bank stopped loaning money, the brothers lost the farm. For young men of the time, there was better money in the city, even in a city as small as Marsden. John and Coop offered sturdy bodies from years of farming, and it was easy for a strong man to find work. People could not tell the twins apart, and as a useful trick, they often traded work. One brother, usually Coop, showed up for work in the morning, and at lunch John replaced him for the remainder of the day. No one was the wiser as long as they wore the same clothes.

Their first job in the city was as rent collectors. The owner of the building knew the many tricks tenants used to dodge the rent collector and he became wealthy collecting rent and ignoring the tricks. After a few years of profit, the owner could hire a strong young man to hammer on doors and collect the money. When he showed up in the owner's office, Coop's size him the job of doing the dirty work. Whether it was Coop working, or John working, either man knew how hard to push to get enough money to satisfy the owner. If it occasionally took a little muscle to frighten a tenant, either of them was up to the task. Their pay was based on commission, so every dollar collected meant more in their pocket.

In that line of work, they also collected stories, told to friends over beer with embellishment and appreciative peals of laughter. Their most popular story happened on a Tuesday in June. Coop was the one who discovered the body, only because it was his day to work, but John would have handled it the same. It was rent day and the old woman who lived in the two-room apartment above 215 Main had been short on her payments for several months. Coop knew her pattern of ignoring his knocks; when he came by at 9:30 a.m., he got no answer. He heard the faint sounds of a radio and was about to leave when he picked up a smell coming from under the door. Coop was no large brain, but even he knew something was wrong. He debated about breaking down the door, but knew the owner would charge him for the door. After some thought, Coop decided to break a window, reach through carefully and open the latch. The window would cost less than the door. As soon as he broke the window, the smell poured out, and he knew something was terribly wrong. He reached through to open the door and followed the smell to the living room. She was in her easy chair in front of the radio, and must have been dead for several days, because of the shiny gray coating over her face where makeup dueled with death for a color. Her lips were curled in a soft smile as if she were grateful to be shed of another bill and to stick it to the owner one last time. Coop opened the door and let the bad air out, left the door ajar, and never told anyone in authority.

In a town as small as Marsden, everyone knew the story by that afternoon. Eventually the police came to talk to Coop to get his story for the record, and he and John had to be careful to get their stories straight. In the retelling, any part of the discovery was fertile material for an embellished story—a story peppered with vivid descriptions of cleverness, the smell, and most vividly, the woman's appearance several days after dying in an unventilated room in the hot summer. The audience was either repulsed or intrigued by the details. Coop got years of story-telling out of the adventure, but eventually everyone had heard it at least once, and his local fame ebbed.

In the 1960's, they decided it was time to give up the bachelor life, settle in town, and become respectable. Land prices were high, except in those areas of town that regularly flooded, with the lowest prices along the town ditch. About this time, John started drinking, sometimes heavily, and that worried Coop because a heavy drinking man is less reliable. They had worked as an effective team for years, each depending on the other to report for work half of the time. They managed to keep their secret of job sharing and were able to save a bit of money to buy land, and Coop did not want to endanger that good situation. The brothers were handy and thought that if they could get a cheap lot, maybe close to the water for a good view, they could manage building a house. This was before urban renewal in Marsden and building codes were not what they are today.

Coop was always on the lookout for property. After considerable scouting, he settled on a stretch of land just along the creek at the end of the town ditch. It was called Sawmill Creek back then. No one wanted the plot as a building site because at least half was overrun with water with every tide. It was slightly higher than swampland. The large triangular lot was bordered by the creek and by the road, and there were no neighbors on adjacent lots. The owners were glad to be rid of it. The brothers bought it for little more than a song and neither of them were good singers. Just after they closed the deal and money had passed hands, they started plans for building their dream house with Coop as the planner and John as the doer; his doing slowed a bit by his afternoon drinking.

Coop started the planning shortly after they had the land. "I know where we can get some red brick for the outside. The planing mill has some beams and lumber we can get pretty cheap. We can wash pilings into this sandy soil and build on the elevated pilings to raise the place above flood level."

"Coop, we just got the land yesterday, no need to start building today. Let's figure out a better way of keeping the land from flooding." John's plan was simple. "Let's bring in truckloads of dirt, spread it around to create a high spot, and build on that big dirt pile. That should put us above the level of the river, even during a hurricane."

For a few weeks, loaded trucks rumbled across the old wooden bridge to dump sandy dirt across the lot. The brothers were out shoveling and leveling till dusk. They were able to raise the main plot to five feet above the creek, with a gentle slope down to the water. Building can be a tricky business, especially for nonprofessionals, and after a short time the brothers disagreed, then started outright fighting. People walking across the bridge could hear their loud arguments and on more than a few evenings, a lot of angry swinging of arms and shovels. It could have been anything that caused the final bitter argument: the strain of hard work, John's drinking, or Coop's demanding attitude. All anyone knows is that one day John was gone and Coop was left to finish.

Coop finished the house of his dreams in a few months and settled into the one story brick building. He married, and his wife loved the house with wonderful views along the creek. Coop's life was fruitful and time passed with children coming, then growing and leaving. A lifetime passed in an instant until Coop's wife became ill and died of cancer. Coop was left alone. He seldom socialized and gradually became more infirm. Eventually, his children convinced him that he needed to move to out of the house because of forgetfulness. His children placed him into the Marsden Town Home when he no longer recognized his family. Everyone seemed happy with the custodial care Coop was able to get in his declining years.

The trouble started early in the summer after the shiny rock became visible at the edge of the creek. Normally creek rocks are angular and mossy, covered in mud, but this one looked different—round, white, and shiny. The creek-side moles did their work all summer and more of the rock was exposed by fall. With tides and water movement, the rock became recognizable as a skull. For some time, it was an undetected skull, because fishermen along the side of Sawmill Creek and on the Main Street bridge could not see it from the angle of the land and it was below the waterline in all but low tide.

According to the official police report, the body was discovered on June 13, 1980. A city worker trimming high grass along the shore stumbled into a mole hole and his foot went into the water. His anger turned to surprise when he looked down and saw the skull staring back at him. The worker jumped out of the water and was so shaken that he had to lay off for the rest of the day. Within an hour, city police were swarming over the sides of the creek. The area was roped off with official yellow crime scene tape and, after the coroner was consulted, digging started. It did not take long to outline the body. By protocol, it remained in place along the muddy creek bed until officials could collect clues that might help with identification. The discovery of a dead body was a morbid attraction in sleepy Marsden. Locals gossiped about the identity of the corpse while they lined up on the bridge to watch the recovery operation. According to the media, the case was being treated as a probable crime, but there was not enough information for the police to make any official comments.

Forensic examiners know that clothes don't wear well on dead people. On a body below ground and enveloped in wet dirt, cotton cloth rots right off, so identifying the remains by clothing was a challenge from the start. One clue in the mystery was quickly reported in the media: the skull was cracked open at the occipital portion and fragments of bone were found inside the skull. Oddly, the body had been laid out in a casual pose, on its back, arms crossed over the chest and legs extended straight, like the person was napping. The pose suggested an intentional moving of the body after death. The gossip was that something bad had happened and that someone had covered it up.

The local crime unit started the investigation, but eventually called in the experts from Raleigh. The chief investigator was interviewed by the local TV station when the story broke and periodically as the investigation continued.

"We know some facts, but not much. We know the body was that of a male, about forty-five years old from bone structure; and we know his skull was crushed, probably by a blunt object. The victim has been dead for more than ten years, but we can't be more specific. It doesn't appear to have been an accident." After the cameras stopped the reporter asked the typical question.

"What else can you tell us?"

"That's it for right now."

"Do you have any suspects, any ideas of what happened?"

"No comment."

Murder is a grisly business, and nothing like this had ever happened in Marsden. Police reassured local residents that the crime was an old one. Nonetheless, nervous neighbors started locking their doors night and day, in case an evil demon might spring out of the bushes beside the creek and whack them a good one up side of their head.

Forensics ran into problems because of the age of the body, and it could not be identified by the usual methods; there was a dental plate, but no dental records; there were no fingerprints, and on and on. Suspicion naturally settled onto the Cooper brothers. In later interviews, the lead investigator added the important piece of evidence that the dirt around the body was different from the usual dirt in that location. Witnesses came forward to report that the Cooper brothers filled the lot with sandy soil just about the time there was a bitter argument between the brothers, and only one brother was accounted for. Unfortunately, Coop was unable to contribute any facts because of his dementia.

Gossips started calling that stretch of creek by the colorful name of "Dead Brother's Creek." Over several years, that name was shortened to Brothers Creek; it was considered to be bad publicity for Marsden to have such a sordid story circulated at a time when town officials wanted to appeal to tourists.

Over a few more years, the case turned cold as no additional evidence was uncovered. Then DNA analysis became an acceptable method for the identification of remains, and an investigator from Raleigh took up the cold case and was able to recover enough DNA from a bone fragment of the skull to run an analysis. Since the Cooper brothers were the prime suspects, investigators visited a seriously-ill Coop and obtained fresh DNA for comparison from his hair and from a mouth swab. No one was surprised when the DNA from Coop and from the skull fragment were an identical match; identical twins have identical DNA. Because John had disappeared many years before after an argument, investigators concluded that the dead resident at the edge of the creek must be John Cooper. The case was closed and no charges were filed because of Coops' medical condition.

For some time, it was news. Shortly after, Coop died. His children found his diary that described that pivotal night. There had been a fight, a silly fight about the placement of a foundation support. John had been drinking and Coop had been especially demanding. Tempers flared and fists flew. In the fight, one brother fell back when his foot wedged into a low spot of dirt and hit his head on an exposed rock. He did not get up. John buried his brother where he'd fallen. It was night by then and he arranged the body in as tasteful a position as he could manage. He took Coop's identity as he'd done so many times before and his life proceeded. The diary ended with the last words, "May he rest in peace. He deserved better" and it was signed by John Cooper.

The story of the diary and the elaborate masquerade was published in papers as far away as Charlotte. A reporter in Raleigh penned the name for that stretch of water between the Main Street Bridge and the Third Street Bridge as Jackson's Creek. Locals feel the name is a fitting memorial to Jackson Henry Anderson Cooper.

Roger and the Jimmylegs

Patrice and I are happily married. We have the occasional disagreement, but after many years together, disagreements come and go after a quick flare. Once things are in the open, issues seem to resolve quickly. I suspect most long-term relationships find this comfortable familiarity. This story is an example of familiarity with a twist that we were lucky enough to discover. If our sensing antennae had not been up, we may have missed an opportunity to deepen our relationship. After all, growth and development are vital.

Our problem is the Jimmylegs. Like most couples, Patrice and I sleep in the same room and in the same bed. A few years ago we got a high-end memory foam mattress, and used a heated mattress pad on cold nights. At a certain age, creature comforts are worth the extra money. The memory foam mattress minimizes the bouncing from the ups and downs during any given night and has proven its worth many times over. Although we rarely go to bed at the same time, neither partner complains when the other comes to bed because the memory foam mattress, like the commercial says, does not spill the wine.

Patrice has always been a restless sleeper. About an hour after she's asleep, unpredictable bouts of Jimmylegs start. Jimmylegs are an unconscious and unexpected jerking of her legs that go for seconds at a time. Patrice sleeps undisturbed through the episodes. Even with the memory foam mattress, I wake up with each jerk. Although the Jimmylegs don't happen every night, they happen often enough. The leg jerks are erratic and intense, but different from the more common Restless Leg Syndrome. Some research suggests that the unconscious movements are a dream response and other research suggests it may be a nervous release of stored muscle energy. Whatever is behind it, the jerking wakes me without fail and I can't get back to sleep. I'm peacefully dozing in near-REM sleep and all of a sudden the covers shake, pull to her side, and a knee jabs me. In her defense, Patrice can't control it. Up until now I've adapted, but recently the restlessness has become more of a thorn in my side. Something needed to be done.

I stewed about it. After three particularly violent nights, I'd had enough and brought up the topic over dinner. The conversation went like this:

"I want to bring up something for discussion; it has to do with our sleeping." I said cautiously.

She looked up from her chicken, a fork midway to her mouth "Sleeping? What do you mean?"

"Your Jimmylegs. We've laughed about them for years, so it's not a new topic."

"Yes," she replied, "and you don't sound as if this is a laughing discussion."

"Well, I don't know why, but now they bother me much more. The bouts are more frequent, and I've not been able to get a sound sleep for weeks. We have to find a way to do something about them. My lack of sleep is going to make me cranky."

"Even more than you are now? Just joking," But she didn't sound all that joking. "What do you suggest?"

"I don't have any quick fixes, after all it's been going on for some time. I just wanted to get your thoughts and let you know I wasn't sleeping well." Maybe my tone here was wrong, because she looked hurt. She looked away and pushed her chair back, perhaps wondering where this topic was headed. I leaned toward her, smiled and continued more gently, "Nothing comes to mind, but let's think about it and talk about it again in a week or so."

Exactly a week passed and Patrice waited till after dinner to start the discussion. "I'm sorry you're not sleeping well, but you know I'm not doing those jerks intentionally and I can't really help what happens when I'm asleep. You've been snoring for years and you can't help that." She pushed away from the table and crossed her arms. "I just don't understand why you're bothered so much all of a sudden and why you just told me about it. Are there other things about me that bother you? Let's get them all in the open as long as we're working on solving problems."

"No, you're nearly perfect, except for the Jimmylegs; and on the snoring, I agreed to try one of those anti-snoring devices, but I haven't. The Jimmylegs bother me more lately. Maybe it's because between the snoring and the Jimmylegs I've not had a good night's sleep in weeks. I'd like to try something."

She listened, but I could tell her mind was analyzing the conversation to see where it might go this time. "Go on."

"I'd like for us to sleep in separate beds for a while to see if it helps me sleep better. I know it's not the perfect solution, but it's the best I can come up with. Separate beds would help get you further away from my snoring."

"Okay," I heard the reluctance come through clearly, as she sat back in the chair and crossed her arms. "I'll try it, but there must be a better solution."

"In my Internet reading over twenty-five percent of couples in relationships over ten years find they sleep better in separate beds, and about five percent find they sleep better in separate rooms. Male snoring seems to be the main issue, and the separate room solution helps the other partner sleep more soundly. Apparently the survey respondents felt that a sound sleep made the world a kinder, gentler place because over seventy-five of them felt the move to separate beds improved their sleep, energy level, and work performance."

Patrice listened and sat quietly, her arms still crossed. She agreed to try separate beds. There was not much talk after that as she cleaned up the dishes. I knew she was thinking of the pros and cons, and I admired her for agreeing in spite of her reluctance.

We shuffled beds and placed the memory foam mattress in the guest bedroom and set up two doubles in our room. They were lower quality mattresses, but this was only a test. The first week was spectacular, and I slept soundly. After two weeks, I was feeling comfortably rested with a new spark of energy, but Patrice was quiet and thoughtful. *Maybe she's not sleeping*, I thought. Over wine one night, she decided to talk about it.

I'd been joking about how much better I was sleeping and that maybe I'd tackle those projects she had on my to-do list. She smiled. "I'd really like that. Some of those have been on the list for a long time. I'm really glad you're sleeping better. You seem to have more energy. I can always tell when you get enough sleep because those dark circles under your eyes are much less noticeable. You even look younger. But, I hope you've noticed that I'm not doing well with this new arrangement." Her smile left and she looked as if she were going to cry.

"I thought you'd be happy for me, for us. What's wrong?"

She continued hesitantly. "I know it's a strange reaction, but I'm feeling rejected. I know rejection is a big emotion, but it's the best I can describe." Tears flowed freely. Patrice doesn't cry often.

My mind processed the word she'd used. Rejection was the furthest thing from my mind, and her tears caught me off guard. No-one had mentioned rejection in the surveys. I tried to get more details. "For most women, sleeping in separate beds lowers the volume of snoring; you've told me before that my snoring keeps you awake."

Tears, then a smile. "That's true, but I've adapted to your snoring. It may sound strange, but after all these years it's soothing and peaceful. I enjoy the rhythm of your breathing. Remember when I mentioned rejection? I looked up the definition to be clear. When I told you I felt rejected, I felt "thrown back" from our communal bed," she said through more tears. "For me, we have a special balance in our relationship and it makes us stronger together. I've always felt that fragile balance is renewed at the close of every day with the simple act of sharing sleep time. We may be separated during the day or may get together for occasional shared talk, but sleep time is our time for peaceful reconnecting at its most basic level. For me it's like a battery recharging, slowly coming up to peak power. Everything else that happens during the day takes a subordinate position to that sleep time. The day closes and we are together. The unspoken reconnection is the most expressive and most silent part of our marriage. I've felt it deepen over our years together and admired that it requires no conscious action. It just happens. You may be surprised, but I feel a special harmony with you in those few moments between half awake and almost asleep." She paused, reluctant to go to the next step after such deep emotions. "Two weeks ago, when we moved into separate beds, we eliminated that closeness and it changed our delicate balance. I've felt it as a loss of something important."

I hadn't thought of it that way, but like a light bulb over a cartoon character's head, it hit me as right on target. I was wrong to leave the bed and thanked her for pointing it out.

I have to add a paragraph explaining the Jimmylegs. The Restless Leg Syndrome is a very real affliction for millions of people, but is not the Jimmylegs we're talking about in this story. RLS occurs primarily at night with not so much uncontrolled jerking, but a sense of crawling, itching, and irritation in one or both legs. For people with RLS, symptoms generally happen while lying in bed. People with RLS may get relief by walking or massaging their legs. There are no specific tests to diagnose the disorder and medication may help only some of the symptoms. Patrice does not have Restless Leg Syndrome in the classical sense, and I doubt there is a medication to prevent her Jimmylegs.

The resolution?

We moved everything back. I probably bother her with my snoring more than she will tell me and she has accepted that. For us it's better for me to adjust to the Jimmylegs. Our talking showed me a side of Patrice I had not known, and I loved her more for sharing it with me. I'm glad to be back enjoying the creature comforts of memory foam and a heated mattress pad. A long body pillow between us works fine for protection.

Roger confronts a turkey vulture

Watching wildlife at the river is an experience at any time of year. I've observed that the duck species are not monogamous and the odd combinations of size and color are a study in genetics. The traditional noisy fanfare of mating in the spring is followed by a proud mother leading her little chicks into their first water experience. The number of chicks tends to drop off to predators day by day, and it's lucky if the most attentive mother can save one or two. Chicks get lost, or more commonly large river turtles pull them down for a meal. Patrice has a soft spot for a little lost duck and its pitiful lonely chirping in the evening.

I came into the natural reality of nature the other morning as I was watching the water and scanning for any new and interesting activity, when I saw a fresh large gull carcass wash up on the beach in front of the house. I use the word *fresh* in that it was new to me, but not knowing how long it had been dead. Circling overhead were three large birds I'd not seen before, and I mistook them for some hawk species. One landed and I identified it as a turkey buzzard by its distinctive ugly red beak. These are impressive birds with a wingspan of over two feet, dark black plumage, and a peculiar and ungainly motion in flight with a kind of rocking motion and more gliding than flapping wings. One of them settled down on the edge of the beach for a meal. I was so intrigued with this encounter that I went out to watch about eight feet from the action. The bird looked at me and hissed (turkey vultures do not have vocal cords, so the best they can do is a low hiss or grunt). He gave me a warning as a second vulture joined the meal. I walked a few steps closer to the carcass just to mess with their minds. The largest turned to confront me and hissed louder in warning. Messing with his mind further I crouched down to make myself more intimidating. The two of them now started hissing loudly and looked like they may be moving into attack mode. The long sharp talons and intimidating curved beak made my decision to stand and walk away. The hissing stopped, and they tore the carcass apart.

I did a bit of online research as they ate. Turkey vultures will commonly regurgitate their meal if they eat too fast or as a protection to lighten their body weight before flight. Apparently I'd created considerable stress. When I came back, there was a bunch of regurgitated gull remains around the carcass and a smell that rivaled what I'd imaged as the contents of opossum stomachs. Readers may wonder how I know that smell, but that's another story.

I'd never seen the vultures at the river before, but then there had not been any potential food as an available carcass either. I took this experience as an interesting encounter with local waterfowl. Turkey vultures are protected under the Migratory Bird Treaty of 1918.

Patrice, the good wife

Women who have been with the same man for ten years or more will find this incident to be pretty typical of men in general. One thing I know about Roger is that he is more than a little tight with his money. It makes me cringe sometimes because that's not my personality, but I have to hold my tongue.

He does not grocery shop often, but when he does; he finds a bargain from Food Lion. Usually the bargain item is close to its expiration date and has one of those orange reduced price stickers. When he gets home, he proudly takes it out of the bag, explains the purchase and wants me to find a way to cook it that night. He calls it creative cooking. I'm as creative as the next person, but there are limits; and sometimes I can get away with freezing and forgetting it.

He came in last Tuesday with large plastic bags filled with two chickens. As an aside, I have to work harder to get him away from using those plastic bags and onto reusable bags, but that's another topic. He was unusually cocky as he told about the great bargain he'd found. The bags contained two large fresh organic roaster chickens of about seven pounds that had been marked down to three dollars each. He told the story with gusto because of some old guy in the checkout line who was eyeing the birds jealously. Roger said their conversation went something like this. (You have to imagine Roger using his own voice and playing the part of the other man with an Eastern North Carolina accent.)

"Pretty nice looking birds," said the man in line. The man was neatly dressed, but Roger said he did not recognize him. Roger likes attention and played up the story it a bit.

"Yep." An unusual response for Roger who is verbose rather than monosyllabic, but he was matching local custom.

"Did you get the last of them?" the man asked. Roger interpreted this as interest in the birds or more likely in the price.

"Yep." Roger said again .

I had to hold back a giggle here because I can picture stiff Roger looking between the chickens and the man, nodding sagely and smiling enigmatically.

"Looks like you're getting a good price on them." The man was surely having some fun with Roger in a gentle Southern way. I had to smile again to think all of this happened in the checkout line. Either the line must have been slow or both of them were chatting and holding up the others in line. I'd have given anything to see the checkout person's assessment of this conversation.

"Yep."

I suspect he was retelling the story for effect and that a lot more happened or it happened a lot quicker.

"There's a lot of meat in those birds, lots more than you get on those hot ones in the case over there; and at a cheaper price, too. I never like the way they cook them in the store. It may be convenient to some, but I like to do it my own way." The man glanced toward the hot food case. Bless his heart for humoring Roger.

"Yep, I like to grill them myself," Roger offered. Just by the way he told it I could tell he was proud of his dialog.

"You having some company over to fix those for?" Now I thought the man had gone over the edge. Then I realized this segment more likely happened after the checkout while they were kibitzing around the shopping carts.

"Nope, just going to cut them up and throw the pieces on the grill. My wife loves my BBQ chicken, and we can get several meals and leftovers out of these big birds."

Well, his BBQ chicken is pretty good, but nothing like Bobby Flay would do on Food Network. I should be glad he went shopping and will be cooking those birds himself rather than having me dream up some creative recipe

"Well, I sure wish I had some BBQ chicken tonight," the man said.

I smiled and wondered if he was angling for a dinner invitation from Roger.

The conversation ended here. I could tell Roger's head was pretty swole from the exchange, that someone had recognized his cleverness in scooping up the last of the birds. I nodded as he took out the birds, turned them over to display their packaging—fresh, never frozen, and organic. He made sure I noticed the bargain price even though he'd told me at least four times that they were bargain birds. Roger likes reinforcement when he has a clever moment, and I nodded with what I hoped was a grateful smile.

We'd had roasters before and because they are larger birds, they tend to be tough, especially when grilled. That's why they're called 'roasters' after all, but I took the high road and didn't mention that.

He no sooner unbagged them than he started cutting them up into grill-size pieces He skinned each piece, something we've discussed for less chicken fat in our diet. As usual, he seasoned them with his special rub, covered them, and left them in the fridge to rest.

He enjoys sitting outside with a cold beer watching the grill heat up and then monitors the flame height after the chicken hits the grill surface. After about forty-five minutes, he brought it in and poured some BBQ sauce over it to rest for the night as we'd planned to have it over the next couple of days. Before bedtime, he sampled a wing.

In the morning over coffee, he gave me an opening. "You may as well just say it now and avoid the waiting."

"What do you want me to say?" This was my response as the good wife.

"Just say I told you so and be done with it," he snapped.

"Great. I told you so, but it's a lot more fun saying it if I know what it's for."

"The chicken is tough and chewy and dry. I probably should have roasted it."

"A good lesson in humility. I told you so." I would have laughed, but he didn't look like he was in the mood.

I guess one definition of a 'bargain' is to actually use the item. Instead, we ordered Oriental food for lunch and not another word was said.

A country healer

All traces of arthritis left Lizzie Hamilton's body on the morning of April 12, 2009. At the start of every New Year, she circled the date on her calendar and sent a silent thank you to James.

"I'm a practical person," she says sheepishly as she recounts the story to her friends. "I don't tolerate any of those superstitious beliefs that are so popular nowadays. Somehow, this is different, and I learned from my own experience that made me believe in superstitions. I used to think that people who believe in healers, fortunetellers, and the like were searching for something that was missing in their lives—a higher power that might intervene to make them better. My thought is that disease, especially a chronic disease, progresses as a foreign affliction visited on a healthy body, and there is no magic about it, just bad luck.

For twenty years, my knees had been getting worse. When I was forty, the slight morning pain in my right knee marched on over the years to a deep pain in both knees that was terrible in wet weather. The pain progressed to both hands, and thankfully became less severe as the day went on. The arthritis was on my mind all the day as I waited for the pain the following morning. That kind of pain and thinking about it took away my energy. My physician offered a variety of medicines to treat the symptoms, but no medicines to cure the arthritis.

Out of curiosity, and my sister's prodding, I had taken to reading articles about alternative medicine. In diseases where traditional medicine fails, many people look for relief in other kinds of medicine. I laughed when I read one article that claimed disease results from an accumulation of bad humors in the body and mind; humors that come from bad living, bad luck, or occasionally as punishment for the bad actions of an ancestor. Now, I don't know about all that in my case, but maybe for some it makes sense.

I grew up in the country around Marsden, my mother used patent medicines from the pharmacists in town and they worked for routine illnesses. In a nod to my mother's beliefs, I tried them all, but nothing did much. My family doctor is a caring healer, but stumped about what to do with the arthritis symptoms. Her trials of medication have just not helped the pain. I was sitting in the doctor's office thinking through my symptoms, weighing the cost of a new medication I had just finished against the slight improvement in morning stiffness, when the nurse called me back for her follow up visit.

Susan Johnston is the new physician in Marsden. I felt she was a good doctor; competent, caring, responsive, and understanding. I told her nurse that the pain was somewhat better during the day, but I was still very stiff in the morning. For the first hour or so, I had to move slowly. She nodded as I told her I had hoped for better pain relief in the mornings. We joked about the cost of medications and what not. The latest one Susan tried cost me over a hundred dollars a month out of pocket.

When Susan asked about the medication, I told her I was pretty much a frail old woman for the first few hours after I get up. By noon, my knees and hands loosen up, and I can move better; but the pain stays on until dinnertime, and then starts again the next morning. She understood when I told her the pain was starting to wear me down. She examined my joints and we talked about her past tests: X-rays did not show severe arthritis, there was no joint destruction and my laboratory studies were normal. Even though she was upbeat about the results, it seemed as if all she could offer were further trials of new and expensive medications and no hope for a cure. The visit ended with my decision to try a less expensive medication for a longer trial period. Susan was a good enough doctor to feel my frustration and I was a sensitive enough patient to feel hers.

As I drove home, I rehashed the challenges: the cost of trials of medications, and further laboratory testing. I had a stack of bills from all those trials. Getting old is hell, but getting old and getting sick is even worse. As

Susan said, on the plus side, the arthritis is not life
threatening; but on the negative side, it hurts a lot every
morning. The only break is if it's a sunny day because
my joints hurt a little less.

My sister, Joanne, has a sympathetic ear for my arthritis
symptoms. Jo is younger and healthier and can offer a
different perspective. Looking up from her coffee cup,
she suggested another approach—seeing a healer. The
man she suggested was not a formal medical man, and
did not use any medicines. People who go to him say he
has a gift. According to Susan's friend Kim, who had
seen him, he doesn't bother much with talking. He
listens carefully to your story on the first visit. After you
finish, he lays his hands on the affected parts, closes his
eyes, and concentrates. Kim was surprised the first time
she went for an ankle sprain because he is one of the few
in the medical field who offered a guarantee. If his
methods don't help what's wrong, he offers to send you
to someone else who has a different gift. If he thinks he
can help, he lays his hands on you again, does his work,
and then sends you home to evaluate the results. If you
are better, you come back and pay him; if not, you don't
have to pay. Jo always has a way of making a story long
and complicated, but she gets the facts right mostly.
When I heard this story, my first thought was that he
must be either a good healer or a poor man.

About a week after my visit with Jo, I'd had enough. It
had been a wet spring season and every morning was a
challenge just to sit up in bed. I called Jo to ask her to go

with me to see the healer. He was in the country past Wilson at a place called Hamilton's Crossroads. There are many Hamiltons in this part of the country, and I didn't know if this crossroad Hamilton was related to us but I took the name as a good omen. For me, crossroads have always had a special significance as a place where different travelers on different roads cross paths for an instant. Interesting coincidences can happen at a crossroads. If strangers happen to cross through at the same time, it's almost as if something was destined to happen. When I drive through a crossroad in the country, I stop, look, and listen for someone who may be coming; someone who might have a part to play in my life. Most times country crossroads are empty, which makes it all the more significant if you meet someone. To me, setting up your business at a crossroads is a good decision; it's convenient with people crossing on their way to somewhere.

His place of business, an ordinary shotgun house with two windows below and two windows above was just like hundreds of houses in Eastern North Carolina. The cream house was neatly trimmed in white, and there were comfortable rockers on the covered porch. It looked like an inviting space where friends could come and visit, rock and talk, and watch whatever was happening on the road in all four directions.

James came out of the back room, introduced himself, and asked me to sit next to him in a rocker. He said he liked to spend most of his visit listening to clients. He did not call them patients, said he never really liked the term because he never did much more than lay hands on them. He only needed a little time to explain what he was doing and why he was doing it. He said that if his power worked for them, the person might be able to better ward off the same disease in the future by knowing how he worked. I guess he was trying to show the person his way of thinking about the world, nature, and disease. His opening speech was calming, because it didn't matter to him if you believed him. He was not trying to convert you and not trying to sell you anything. He was offering his gift to whoever came through his door; you could choose to take or not take it. I didn't ask him how many of his clients left before he did anything, or even how many people got better and stayed better. That was his secret, I guess.

We moved to the front room and arranged ourselves across from each other, and he asked why I had come. I told the story of the arthritis as accurately as I could and he listened quietly, nodding when I came to the parts about trying different medications and them not working. I must have been a good historian, because he only nodded occasionally to encourage me to keep telling the story. He watched me with his careful eyes as if he had all the time in the world. When I finished, he smiled and thanked me for being so accurate; he said it made his job easier if a person was a careful observer. He asked to see my wrists and to move them around. It was close to noon by that time, so they were not too stiff but still painful. I was wearing slacks and he never asked to see my knees where the whole business started, which surprised me. After watching me move my wrists and gently feeling the bones on down to my fingertips, he sat back in his chair.

I remember his words because they told me more than the doctors had told me. 'The arthritis has settled pretty strong in your bones. You say it's worst in your knees and wrists, some in your fingers?'

I nodded.

He claimed that the bones didn't feel damaged like other folks he'd seen with deformed joints set on by destructive arthritis. He nodded to me as he said how it's almost impossible to bring damaged joints back to normal. He felt my kind of arthritis was more hopeful. According to him, a fire had settled into the bones and it was just a matter of drawing it out to get rid of the symptoms. Once the fire was gone, the bones would heal themselves. He asked if I wanted him to try to remove the fire.

I told him to do what he needed to do. Something about him made me trust him to do what was best.

He smiled, and started to explain about his healing techniques. It was a simple explanation. His gift, as much as he understood it, was to draw power from water or sometimes from the earth. In my case, moving water was best and the faster it was moving, the stronger his power. A waterfall is best for severe disease, but there aren't any in Eastern North Carolina, so he had to be content with a stream. He said he used to live next to a fast stream, but with hurricanes and flooding, that stream destroyed his house three times.

He asked if I was well enough to walk to a small stream behind the house. He wanted to draw out the fire using something that lives in the earth, a green stick or a smooth stone freshly dug from the earth. He found a stone in the mud of the stream, about as big as the palm of his hand, and held it against my right wrist for a minute or so before tossing it into the moving water. He claimed the flowing water diluted the pain. To prevent the arthritis settling back, he poured some water over my wrist in order to restore the balance. He said it took him several years to learn that pouring water right away was essential so that the body could take on some of the power of the water and keep the fire away.

He smiled as we stood and explained that he felt good about the disease leaving and that by the morning I should have only a little stiffness that would go away as my body rebalanced. We walked back to the house and up the stairs to the porch. He invited me to sit a while, and the porch was so inviting that Jo and I sat while I took notes.

As I talked with Jo on the drive home, we smiled at how different this was from a doctor's visit. Being with him made me feel brighter, like a sunny day after a storm or a perfect sunset. I wasn't the least bit surprised when I was much better the next morning. Over the next few days there was no stiffness in the morning. The arthritis never came back.

About a week later, I went back to pay him for his good work. There was no one at the house, but I slid a check through the mail slot. How do you decide how much to pay someone for such a profound service? I settled on the amount of money I saved on medication each month because of his help. I knew the amount really didn't matter. I've not gotten back that way in some time and wonder if he's still in that house at the crossroads. Friends are surprised by the story and wonder if he can help their problems, but I never knew if they went to see him. I thank him every morning in my prayers, but especially on the anniversary of my first visit to his house at the crossroads. He is one good man trying to do good work for people, an unusual happenstance in this busy world.

Roger judges the Chili Cook-Off

In Eastern North Carolina the tradition of roasting a
whole pig must have deep roots in history. The ritual of
patience, sitting with friends and the frequent brushing
with a chili-vinegar sauce, are choreographed with lots
of beer. It's a man's task.

In Marsden, the festival event of the fall, Smoke Over
the River, offers two widely different culinary events:
the Pig Cooking Contest and the Chili Cook-off. One is
for professionals and the other is for local professionals.
The Pig Cooking Contest is the main event with well-
established rules, pageantry, a parade of pig-cooking
apparatus and the sale of BBQ-related paraphernalia.
The contest draws the best cooks from the region
looking for the $1,500.00 first prize and bragging rights.

My passion is chili. In Boston, chili is on dinner tables
across the city during the cold winter months. I've tried
many recipes and consider myself a connoisseur. Patrice
and I have been to parties in Boston where a lively
disagreement might erupt over the pros and cons of a
tomato-based sauce. At Smoke Over the River there is a
Chili Cook-off almost as an afterthought to the Pig
Cooking Contest; but in my mind, it's the highlight. The

organizers make a point that the event is not sanctioned by the Chili Appreciation Society International. Who knew there were organizations with international rules on cooking chili? An advantage of not being sanctioned, in my opinion, is a more freewheeling contest with local color and only a few general guidelines, mostly involving sanitation.

A contestant team can enter up to two chili recipes for the forty dollar entry fee, and the event takes place rain or shine. Often there is rain and wind on the waterfront and chili is perfect to warm you up a cold day. The chili is cooked at home and a three gallon cooking container is brought in for judging. Some teams opt for decorative side items of crackers, cheese, onions, or like food items that add punch and appeal to the judges. The finished product is assessed by three judges on TACA (taste, aroma, consistency, and aftertaste).

Before the Noon Rotary started managing the cook-off, it was a casual event. Regular judges were local celebrities who hated to miss a chance to wax eloquently on chili. Several years ago, I was surprised and honored to be one of the three judges. Now, truth be known, one of the real judges had other commitments and I was a last-minute substitute. My lack of celebrity status or chili experience didn't faze me in the least. I know chili the most authentic way, from experience.

A good chili judge arrives well before the 10:00 a.m. judging. Wandering around is not allowed for fear of discovering who is associated with any chili. Nonetheless, I wanted to be prepared for my first judging; so at 7:30 a.m., I was walking along the festival midway to feel the atmosphere. Food and craft vendors were sipping their coffee and setting up booths while they repositioned signs downed in the wind the night before.

The sun was coming up on a crisp fall morning with a Carolina blue sky. By nine the chili tent was bustling with contestants and volunteers. This year there were thirteen contestants arranged on side tables with their pots and sides displayed as artfully as allowed. The contestants chattered along doing final tasting and adjustments. An overwhelming aroma of roasting pig drifts over in the gentle breeze.

I met my fellow judges and they politely nodded. I had some cautious thoughts about eating thirteen sample bowls of chili that early but felt I was up to the task. My fellow judges, veterans, listened to the rules as they had each year. We were given a grading sheet to score on TACA with the interpretation left to our individual palates. I didn't want to be a slouch on rules and protocol, so I'd been to the website the night before to check out the International Chili Society (ICS) rules for chili competitions and descriptions of what TACA entailed. I'd cooked up a few batches of Boston chili the week before, and Patrice was getting pretty tired of chili for lunch and dinner. I could tell she was humoring me when I pressed for her thoughts on taste and aroma. She can tolerate chili about once a month in cold weather, less so in the hotter months. She complains that I make too much and we have three days of chili leftovers to finish; but to me, making less than a gallon of chili is a waste of energy. Small batches lose the subtlety of the spices.

Judges are seated separated from contestants, backed up to the cooking tables. My plumber found out I was judging and gave me a friendly smile just the day before at Lowe's. He is one of the regular contestants. I was determined to remain unbiased and did not ask about his experience.

Each contestant's chili is delivered by the organizer in a four-ounce paper cup. My fellow judges made a show of tasting, washing the chili around in their mouth, and marking a grade on their card. I took a novel approach. My method was to taste one small spoonful and set the remaining chili on the table in front of me. The procession of chili cups continued from red to white to vegetarian to extra spicy with beans, no beans, hearty chunks of meat, coarsely ground meat, chicken, pork, beef, and tofu.

The veterans treated each cup the same and graded each within thirty seconds. I was alone using the small-taste-technique. That method was considerably slower. My plan was to sample each cup then come back and compare different closely-associated flavors and textures and finally settle on the best. While this was a logical plan, it was agonizingly slow. A half hour passed. The competitors were getting antsy, and the organizers were getting nervous. Everyone was ready to roll along with chili sales since the real goal was to sell chili and donate the profits to charity. I was holding up the sales process.

I worked through my line of cups again and grouped similar flavors before excluding some of the thirteen. My fellow judges watched with smirks, because they had already turned in their cards and were enjoying this display. I narrowed the cups down to eight, then five, then three and took particular care to rank those final three with my last spoonfuls. If I'd have been a regular judge, I would have tasted those final three with satisfying sounds of chili pleasure. I thought that kind of behavior was too over the top, and so I just looked thoughtful. I entered scores for those three and turned in my card, satisfied I'd done the best I could. The organizer breathed a sigh of relief and started getting the volunteers ready for sales.

The chili sold at the booth that year was from each competitor until it was gone, then a generic chili was made on the spot. You'd be surprised how many people like chili for a late morning snack. Most customers also carried a BBQ sandwich in a greasy bag for lunch. A fine time was had by all; but after thirteen cups of chili, I needed some antacid.

At the afternoon presentation, the winner was my plumber, fair and square.

After that one time, I've not been asked back as a judge, but I can hope. My lesson on local custom was that it's better to follow the example of experienced judges and move right along with your responsibility. It's only chili after all.

Rose's fried chicken

Met loves fried chicken and will make necessary social sacrifices to have fresh chicken cooked perfectly. The anatomy of the bird is not important, because white meat and dark meat have an equal place in his heart. Met will travel across town to taste a steaming plate of golden chicken, but he doesn't have to go even that far. Rose fixes the best chicken he's ever tasted, and she lives just down Main Street. Her friends believe she has an unrequited romantic interest in Met, but no one knows if her interest is in the present or in the future or whether Met is privy to her plan. On his side, he believes in the friends-with-benefits philosophy and Rose's fried chicken is the benefit. Rose invites him over for chicken irregularly during the month and sends word through his friends that he should come on such-and-such a date and time. No matter what else is going on, he never misses those appointments.

Rose prepares fresh chicken by carefully trimming away the fat and deboning each piece; a time-consuming process. This method makes each piece true finger food without any bones to work around. Met knows deboning fried chicken is not traditional for a Southern woman; but once he tasted her recipe, he was in love and thoughts on tradition went by the wayside. She lovingly massages each piece with a special spice mix before resting the pieces in the fridge for an hour or so to let the spices work their magic before breading. Removing the skinny wing portion improves frying. Without those scraggly wing ends, the pieces of one chicken fit nicely into her large cast iron pan. She works with care and timing because she knows he will be on time.

He arrives freshly washed and shaved, and Rose smiles up at him as she opens the front door. Her house is small and neat with everything painted a soft cream. The front door is an oddity from a previous owner, sturdy mahogany painted over many times, and one tiny window too high to be functional for her to see who might be on the other side. She's a short sturdy woman who has to crack the door to see who's knocking, but Cole is so tall she can see his face through the window.

Met sits in the large red chair in the corner of the parlor, and she sits opposite with the light behind to soften her features. She offers iced tea, and he accepts. Introductory polite chat and local news fill any awkward time, and then she moves the questions to his health and what he's been doing—inquiring talk carefully spoken to avoid the impression of prying. What conversation there is comes from her. He answers with short direct replies, glancing at her face after each question. During the gentle waves of talk he crosses his long legs and dangles his left foot, tapping it gently while deciding how to answer. She reads the tapping as nervousness and notes the cadence. The more she asks about his comings and goings, the faster his foot taps. Careful as he is to modulate his foot, he cannot stop the movement; and like a poker tell, his foot betrays his nervousness about personal details. She varies her questions so as not to overly direct attention to his personal side, a technique she's learned from experience with Southern men. After a suitable social time, she nods, satisfied with the information, and retires to the kitchen. As she leaves, he sips his tea, alone and quiet, and his foot is still.

The dining room is beside his chair, and he sees her bring rolls and a dish of slaw before neatly arranging the table. He hopes she'll have the butter beans he loves, prepared with just a bit of crunch and tenderness. Through the door he can hear her bustling in the kitchen, softly humming a tune as she fries the chicken. When the chicken is to her liking, she brings the aromatic plate to the table with what she hopes is a flourish. After she sits, she bows her head and extends her right hand; he takes it and she intones a blessing of company, food, and friendship. During prayer, he gently squeezes her hand and sits straight-backed waiting for her to finish. Rose smiles at him after she's spoken a soft amen and continues holding his hand for several breaths as she looks to him for approval.

She never eats when he eats, but watches him eat his fill, usually four pieces. She catches her breath watching the breading stick to his fingers and loves his smile as he licks the crunch off his index finger and thumb. He favors the juicy meat of deboned thighs and has a special fondness for the Pope's nose. That end piece of fat has an extra burst of flavor and he always saves it for his last bite. During the meal he wipes his fingers on her cloth napkin out of politeness and smiles often because he senses it pleases her.

The interplay of each visit is the same. As he finishes, he looks into her eyes with what he hopes is appreciation and verbally thanks her. She's learned the softly mouthed words are his signal that he's preparing to leave. The whole affair lasts perhaps ninety minutes; more often closer to sixty. Rose tries to be efficient in the preparing and serving to respect the time he's giving. She would like more of his time after the meal, but respects his timetable. Tonight there is less conversation than she needs, but Met is a private man and slow to share his emotions. Rose hopes the dinner appeals to him, and that he will talk more at a later dinner. Although she would like for him to stay longer, she never insists. She often tries to entice him to stay with fresh pie; occasionally, the conversation starts again over the pie. Those conversations are easier and more relaxed. She feels he is relating to her.

When he is ready to leave, he stands, stretches, and rubs his stomach. He holds his arms out to her. She comes into his open arms and he enfolds her. His right hand holds the tip of her chin and delivers one soft kiss to her cheek. She smiles as he releases her. He sniffs the chicken on his fingers and walks into the night.

As far as anyone knows, Met is her only beau. Rose is a good woman, and Met knows he does not deserve her caring. Neither of them has yet found a way to change the pattern. For Rose, it had been different with her last beau. He was more talkative. Rose felt she drove him away by being too clingy and demanding more than he could give. She tries to avoid that mistake this time.

Patrice goes to the beach

All my life I've been a fiddler. Since we retired, it's become more noticeable. After retirement, Roger took the lead in finding projects for himself, and I didn't know what I wanted to do, so I fiddled. It's been my experience that if I fiddle around long enough, without fretting or nagging myself, I'll find the next right thing to make me happy. I don't worry about how happiness might come, except to feel that eventually I'll immerse in it and it would feel right.

On a Monday morning, the spring weather was warm and the breeze was refreshing. There had been swarms of fuzzybills clustered around the screens last night. In my reflective times, the most calming place is watching the darkness settle over the water and the clouds drift gray across the sky, but the hum of fuzzys disturbed any reflective time. There has to be a way of calming them in the spring.

I needed some time away. Roger is a fine man and always seems to find things to keep him busy, but when people are retired and don't have much that needs to get done, they get to irritating each other. We were getting to the edge of my patience with him. Disengagement was the best choice, and the beach the perfect location. I asked Lizzie to come along, but she's not a beach person, so I drove alone to Kitty Hawk. The beach in the summer is not for me; crowds, sand, heat, children, and bugs don't appeal to me.

I like the beach in the fall when the sand is empty for long stretches. Brisk weather and a cool breeze on a nice fall day are exhilarating and thought-provoking. Walking along the sand with the steady background lap of the waves gives a body time to think. My hair does better in the fall, and I don't come away with that finger–in-the-electric-socket look. There is no need for beachwear or fancy cover-ups. Sweaters cover most of the signs of age, yet allow a casual and stylish look. No one stops to talk and the open sand stretching beyond the water line encourages walking and reflecting.

The sun was bright with a brisk easterly breeze. Walking along the dry sand in my bare feet felt healthy, testing muscles that were not normally used. My thoughts turned to evaluating my life to date and looking for answers. I needed contentment and therapy for the soul. I took a notebook to jot down any insights; if these notes seem a bit random, that's how the thoughts came. Sharing the thoughts just seems like a completion and a nudge to action.

My first question, patterned by my mother, Marta, is always: how have I done in life? Following quickly, in no particular order, are the stock questions everyone asks.

Am I a good wife to Roger? Will I ever be famous? Will I be inspired to write a grand successful novel? Will I be a guiding light for some wayward soul, my guidance setting them on the path to goodness? The packed sand gives just enough under my footsteps to beat a rhythm, crystallizing my questions into organization. The smell of the ocean kept those thoughts alive, reforming them into further practical exploration of what talents I've used.

In my walks, the first idealistic thoughts always evolve to practical questions. Roger. Unless he gets moving, bless his soul, he won't ever achieve much success, if there is such a thing as success in retirement. He keeps trying by following ambitions he talked about so many years ago, and I admire him for persistence. Maybe I'm different and at peace with letting old dreams pass on.

How is retirement for me? Is it the beginning of the end, a waiting time? No. Overall, retirement has been good. Our social encounters in Marsden are as a couple. When he worked, Roger had a tendency to be overbearing in social situations. Since he retired and does not need to butt heads with other men, he seems calmer in social situations. A recent oyster roast comes to mind. If he starts down the familiar road of righteous authority, I flash "the look" and that is all that's needed. At home, he knows enough to back off when I have had enough, so we've reached a stable, peaceful time together. I'm thankful we have that peace when so many other couples are in friction during retirement.

In school, I was taught to strive to live a good life. What is a good life? Maybe manifesting the best values we learned in childhood of honesty, hard work, helping those less well off, trusting our leaders, and a daily effort to improve things in our own little world. Sounds pretty sappy when I put it on paper, but it was not sappy on the beach walk. I felt a 60's feeling flow into me— optimism. Anyway, what's so wrong with sappy?

During retirement, I feel a different sense of time. When I worked, every hour had a meeting, a deadline, or some task that demanded attention. Time flew by. Now, time is a gentle stream that flows over me. Occasionally an interesting piece of material floats by in the stream, but the urgency to chase it is gone. I'm more content to just watch it float by. I'm not sure if that is good or bad, it just is.

How is my life in general? Overall, pretty good. My answer as if I was checking a box on an evaluation form. We are able to do joint projects around the house and continue our remodeling of the river place, knowing we might never get it exactly right. If I did not come up with ideas, poor Roger would be off on his own tangents and nothing would get done. We have both been healthy (my superstitious side says not to write about good health as health can change quickly). A friend once told me the best laugh God has is when we tell him our plans. I guess health is doing what you can do for yourself and hoping for the best. Both Roger and I do a moderate amount of exercise, but he does not do it easily. I suspect he loafs when I send him to the treadmill, because he never comes back with even a light glow of sweat. Of course, we feel individual muscle aches more than we did twenty years ago. I smile when others catalog on which muscles ache from which activity. Every morning we both creak a bit getting up. Roger is up several times during the night because his prostate is not what it used to be. I've started him on pumpkin seed capsules. No verdict yet on whether that will help. Like so many natural products today, ground pumpkin seed is advertised as rich in omega fatty acids and an ancient remedy for American Indian elder males. So far the pumpkin hasn't had a dramatic effect on Roger.

Maybe this is all part of my fiddling. I will find my rhythm in Marsden. Reading *Sound-Off* is my morning joy with publication of the opinion of small-town America. When I scan the events listed for the week, I remember my hope of joining a group of women for girl sessions. So far, I've not found the group that speaks to me. Truth be known, I have not been as good a searcher as I should. Most of my day involves giving Roger the attention he needs to stay on an even keel. My mother would mock that it's a sad way to spend my golden years. An unexpected large wave hits and the cold water creeps up the sand to my feet, mother laughing.

I enjoy cooking, visiting with friends, and mining the social side of Eastern North Carolina. I use mining because it's sometimes a challenge to dig out the opportunities. Like any small town, Marsden can be cliquish. But more and more, I sense there is something undiscovered here. I have not (yet) found a passion, something that might consume large quantities of energy. I admire my friends who have found their passion of gardening, quilting, scrap-booking, or volunteering. I see an artistic side somewhere deep down, but it hasn't matured yet. I smile at the ocean asking, what am I waiting for, a lightning strike from above?

Could my passion be on the stage? Amateur theater has possibilities in Marsden. Still, one does not just fall into stage parts without some training. Singing is out but painting has possibilities. I laugh at that old TV show with the guy who showed us all how to paint nature scenes with happy little trees. Unfortunately, he died and I don't want to buy the old DVD badly enough to get into happy trees. But then, I guess you have to break a few eggs and keep refining the recipe before the cake gets better, so I'll try a bit of painting. What am I waiting for?

I'm coming to the fishing pier as my northern boundary and turn to start back. This time the breeze is in my face, and I can feel and smell the salt air even more. There is a couple on the beach holding hands. The walk back is more relaxed, watching the gulls and feeling the power of the waves. No relaxing walks like this were available in Boston.

Time slipped by on the walk back, as if the questions had already resolved, and I was soon back at the car. The oysters at Basnights were fantastic, lightly breaded and lightly fried. Somehow having that pep talk with myself helped reset my balance and I drove home happy. I'll call the college tomorrow and see if there are volunteer openings in set design. What will Roger say?

About the Author

I've been a listener nearly all of my life. As a physician, listening was essential to making an accurate diagnosis; it was natural. As I listened to patients and friends, more people chose to share stories. Listening to them showed a bit more of the culture of Marsden.

This collection started years ago as a back porch conversation with a fisherman in coastal North Carolina. Other stories were added and evolved into a collection that I hope reflects the uniqueness and diversity of the people of Marsden. Each of these stories started with a kernel of truth, bouncing around until the finished story was ready to come out onto the page.

A combination of luck, encouragement from writing enthusiasts and a period of enforced inactivity was the push needed to finish.

My interest includes medical carpentry: a merging of medicine, computer art, and carpentry. My favorite project is creating finger labyrinths for relaxation therapy in patients. I've donated the labyrinths to autistic children and chemotherapy patients to help them relax. Check out my travel blog at http://year-of-adventure.typepad.com/yearofadventure/ for more on the labyrinth project.

Look for a follow up collection of stories about Roger and Patrice and the other characters as they live their lives in Marsden. Contact me at Knowledgeworks123@gmail.com.

30461471R00112